D0987235

GREAT ·MILITARY LEADERS

Joan of Arc

Kristin Thiel

Cavendish Square

Published in 2018 by Cavendish Square Publishing, LLC
243 5th Avenue, Suite 136, New York, NY 10016

First Edition

Website: cavendishsq.com

This publication represents the opinions and views of the author based on his or her personal
experience, knowledge, and research. The information in this book serves as a general guide
only. The author and publisher have used their best efforts in preparing this book and disclaim
liability rising directly or indirectly from the use and application of this book.

CPSIA Compliance Information: Batch #CS17CSQ

All websites were available and accurate when this book was sent to press.

Library of Congress Cataloging-in-Publication Data

Names: Thiel, Kristin, 1977- author.
Title: Joan of Arc / Kristin Thiel.
Description: New York : Cavendish Square Publishing, 2018. | Series: Great
military leaders | Includes bibliographical references and index. |
Description based on print version record and CIP data provided by
publisher; resource not viewed.
Identifiers: LCCN 2017007396 (print) | LCCN 2017006692 (ebook) | ISBN 9781502627919
(library bound) ISBN 9781502627926 (E-book)
Subjects: LCSH: Joan, of Arc, Saint, 1412-1431--Juvenile literature. |
Christian women saints--France--Biography--Juvenile literature. |
Christian saints--France--Biography--Juvenile literature. | Women
soldiers--France--Biography--Juvenile literature. |
Soldiers--France--Biography--Juvenile literature. |
France--History--Charles VII, 1422-1461--Juvenile literature.
Classification: LCC DC103.5 (print) | LCC DC103.5 .T54 2018 (ebook) | DDC
944/.026092 [B] --dc23
LC record available at https://lccn.loc.gov/2017007396978150262

Editorial Director: David McNamara
Editor: Molly Fox
Copy Editor: Rebecca Rohan
Associate Art Director: Amy Greenan
Designer: Jessica Nevins
Production Coordinator: Karol Szymczuk
Photo Research: J8 Media

The photographs in this book are used by permission and through the courtesy of: Cover, 19, 79 PHAS/UIG/Getty Images;
p. 4 Graphica Artis/Hulton Archive/Getty Images; p. 8 Hilary Jane Morgan/Perspectives/Getty Images; p. 12 Interfoto/Alamy
Stock Photo; p. 16 Buyenlarge/Archive Photos/Getty Images; p. 27 Ivy Close Images/Getty Images; p. 28 Alessia Pierdomenico/
Shutterstock.com; p. 30 traveler1116/iStockphoto.com; p. 33 Josse Christophel/Alamy Stock Photo; p. 37 Jeanne d'Arc entend
des voix/Bridgeman Images; p. 41 Ken Welsh/Perspectives/Getty Images; p. 44, 46, 70, 104 De Agostini Picture Library/Getty
Images; p. 54-55 Hulton Archive/Getty Images; p. 59 duncan1890.iStockphoto.com; p. 62 Leemage/Corbis/Getty Images; p. 68-
69 Fine Art Images/Heritage Images/Getty Images; p. 72 H. Armstrong Roberts/ClassicStock/Getty Images; p. 76-77 Universal
History Archive/UIG/Getty Images; p. 83 Jean-Sebastien Evrard/AFP/Getty Images; p. 85 Scott Nelson/AFP/Getty Images; p. 90
Photo12/UIG/Getty Images; p. 92 Historical Picture Archive/Corbis/Getty Images; p. 97 (left) M. Seemuller/DeAgostini/Getty
Images, (right) Bettmann/Getty Images; p. 99 EDimages/Alamy Stock Photo; p. 106 Starryvoyage/Shutterstock.com; p. 108
Alfred Eisenstaedt/The LIFE Picture Collection/Getty Images.

Printed in the United States of America

TABLE OF CONTENTS

The Demonized, Celebrated National Hero

Joan of Arc's story is inspirational and heartbreaking. Born in the medieval French countryside and living to be only nineteen years old, Joan experienced an expansive life that feels mystical by modern standards. It involved deep spiritual faith, bloody battles, and a gory death. She has become a religious icon, a feminist hero, a symbol of nationalism, and a misunderstood and mislabeled object of ridicule.

Joan believed that she was in direct communication with God, that he'd chosen her for a special, monumental role, and that the words of his messengers, given directly and specifically to her, would guide her, her country, and her religion to glory over a long-hated enemy.

Despite having no military training, and despite being a female in a male-dominated society, Joan convinced French royalty to let her command a unit in a battle against the country's longtime enemy, England. To complicate matters, France's

Opposite: Frank E. Schoonover's 1918 imagining of Joan of Arc shows her leading her men into battle, her sword raised.

allegiances were divided at the time, and when Joan went into battle against England, she was also fighting some of her French countrymen, the Burgundians. Joan stood strong in her divine convictions. Under her leadership, her men won, more than once, against the English and the Burgundians.

This national joy turned into personal horror: Joan was captured by Anglo-Burgundian forces, imprisoned, and tried for crimes against both God and the state. For a year, she lived in a cell, her every word and action picked apart by men more than twice her age. Again, she stood strong—she was smart, she was savvy, and she was unruffled—but she could not win against this enemy. She was convicted of the charges and burned at the stake in 1431.

Joan's story doesn't end even with such a terrifying, dramatic death, though. In a sense, she rose again nearly five hundred years after her death, when the Roman Catholic Church **canonized** her as a saint in 1920. In society's eye, she went from curiosity to hero; then, she became an immoral heathen. Finally, she rests holding the title of a revered person.

What's amazing is that modern civilization knows of her story at all. She was a country girl born not only six hundred years before the minute-by-minute chronicling of social media, but two decades before the first use of the printing press in Europe. Under normal circumstances, her story would not have been recorded, let alone saved and shared for generations. But, of course, these weren't normal circumstances. Her voice, along with the voices of the many people who knew her personally and professionally, can be experienced through reading the transcript from her 1431 trial. Records still exist from the trial held in 1456 to clear Joan's name, also.

Still, there are many reasons mystique surrounds her. These records can feel inaccessible and untrustworthy. They're written in **clerical** Latin, so there is, at the least, the distance imposed by translation of the French people spoken into the archaic language of record. As early as 1452, people questioned the record: the English, Joan's captors, were vehemently biased against her, likely threatening everyone associated with her trial, down to the notaries, to twist the record against her. Joan was uneducated and young—was it right that she had been made to stand trial alone? It's impossible to read through the transcripts and settle easily on a single consistent story about what happened and who Joan was.

Whomever Joan was and whatever the details of her life, nothing about is ordinary, yet what rises to the top of an incredible list is the extraordinary way society received her. Joan was the golden child—until she wasn't. The men who thought they were in charge of her—sexism was clearly at play here— accepted her when it served them to do so and persecuted her when they needed to. Her life of kings and holy messengers may sound otherworldly now, but the reaction to her feels all too real still today.

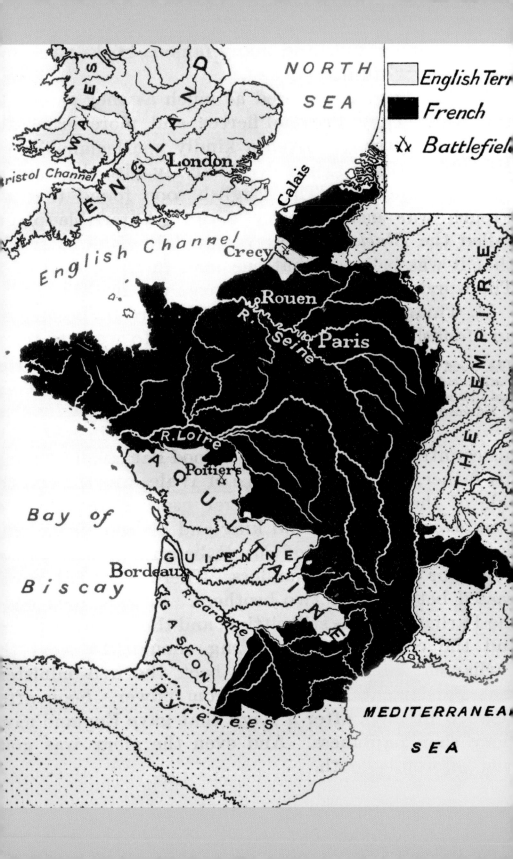

NORTH SEA

English Terr[itory]

French

Battlefiel[d]

WALES

ENGLAND

London

Bristol Channel

Calais

English Channel

Crecy

Rouen

R. Seine

Paris

THE EMPIRE

R. Loire

A
Q
U
I
T
A
I
N
E

Poitiers

Bay of

Biscay

GUIENNE

Bordeaux

R. Garonne

G
A
S
C
O
N
Y

Pyrenees

MEDITERRANEAN

SEA

CHAPTER ONE

The Culture *of* Medieval France

J oan never knew a world without war. When she was born, France and England were in the middle of what historians starting in the 1800s would call the Hundred Years' War (1337–1453). During the Middle Ages, people probably just saw it as more fighting, indistinguishable from the fighting before and blurring into the fighting that came after. Joan's country had been engaged in simmering disagreement or outright battle with England for centuries by the time she was born and would continue to be for centuries after her death. What was unique about the war of Joan's time was that it was a total war, the line between military and citizenry blurred. Because taxes, officially collected and unofficially stolen, funded the military, if the opposing military attacked its enemy's people, that also meant an attack on the opposing country's military resources. Church bells ringing could mean a call to worship or a raid on the town.

Opposite: This map shows the English presence in France after the Treaty of Calais in 1360.

Joan also only knew a world in which spiritual commands were to be taken as seriously as earthly laws. God's will determined what happened: if you were rewarded, you were in God's favor; if you experienced a downfall, he was angry at you. A person could channel God's, or the devil's, words. Within all this, women and men held different stations in society. Men held political and clerical power, and women could be cast as pawns of war and conduits for the devil. This **thought-world** provides a broad structure for how and why Joan's experiences came to be.

Women and Religion

Among the voices Joan of Arc heard were those of female visionaries who had come before her, including Saint Catherine and Saint Margaret. In the Middle Ages, women could also hold leadership roles within the church.

Catherine of Alexandria, Who Became Saint Catherine

Unlike Joan's story, which is supported by surviving historical record, Catherine of Alexandria's story offers no proof from primary sources. There are only memories, passed down the generations, of her birth around the year 287 CE into a noble, maybe even royal, family in Egypt. Like Joan, Catherine held fast to her faith, even through torturous questioning and death.

At about fourteen years old, she saw a vision of the Virgin Mary and Jesus and converted to Christianity, a dangerous decision at that time. Roman Emperor Maxentius was actively persecuting Christians.

Boldly, Catherine went to him and challenged him. Rather than executing her on the spot, as he very well might have, he summoned fifty experts to debate her. Imagine their terror, especially when some gathered there were moved by her words to convert, and were immediately hauled off and killed.

Eventually tired of this game, Maxentius ordered her imprisoned. Catherine resisted the torture through faith, she said, and when news of this spread, she began receiving amazed visitors, hundreds of them, at her cell.

Eventually, in the year 305, the emperor ordered an end to all of it. Catherine was to be executed. They took her to the spiked breaking wheel, a device reserved for killing the worst criminals. Before they could attach Catherine to it, it broke. Enraged, Maxentius ordered her simply beheaded.

The Catholic Church canonized her as a saint, but there's no reference of her before the ninth century. There were a lot of references to her during Joan's time—during the medieval era, Catherine was one of the most popular saints.

Margaret of Antioch, Who Became Saint Margaret

There is even less known about St. Margaret than there is about Catherine, but she too was an immensely important saint to those living in Joan's time.

Born in what is now Turkey, Margaret was cast out of her house by her pagan **priest** father when she converted to Christianity. Out in the world, she angered a local leader with her faith, and he had her tortured and imprisoned and then attempted to execute her first by burning, then by drowning, and finally by beheading.

The story that spread during the Middle Ages was that during her imprisonment the devil visited her in the form of a dragon. He swallowed her, but the cross in her hand scratched his throat, and he coughed her out, still alive.

Abbesses

An abbess, the female head of a monastery of nuns, broke gender constrictions of the day by assuming legal, **ecclesiastical**, and spiritual leadership duties that otherwise were allowed only to men. She was, in essence, a "female father." As part of their secular duties, abbesses could be in charge of entire counties, at least to make minor decisions for them. The degree of their authority was constantly under review by male clerics, but abbesses did hold a unique power.

Women in Society

To explain how teenage Joan was received by men and women alike, it's also helpful to understand their roles in society.

Women as Landowners

A woman could receive land through inheritance or marriage. Though marriage placed any inherited estate holdings under her husband's control, the woman still could find herself in charge. Christine de Pisan's *Book of the City of Ladies*, written around 1405, was the first women's history book written by a woman. It offered the advice that women should know how to administer

Opposite: This illustration, from around 1880, shows Margaret and the dragon she saved herself from.

their properties because their husbands would so often be absent. By the early 1400s, formal education was encouraged for women likely to inherit land—that is, for the wealthy.

Adolescence

Social adolescence didn't start to be treated as a phase of life until Joan's time. Before then, people started training for careers before puberty and in many circumstances, could inherit property and live on their own once they were in their mid-teens. Then, universities were developed, lengthening the schooling years, and lawmakers raised the age at which a person could be independent. Writers began describing youth as a time for freedom from responsibility. These changes affected males more than females. For example, females were still married off at young ages and therefore expected to behave as adults.

Paris

Paris was a mess at this time, alternately fought over and forgotten. When Henry V rode triumphantly into the city on December 1, 1420, children were literally dying in the streets from hunger. In stark contrast to the people's reality, during this celebration, wine ran without stopping from the public water conduits.

In the summer of 1425, the city was in a state of neglect by the powerful, and one Parisian's surviving journal reported two diversions, which highlight if not what passed for entertainment for all people in the 1400s, at least what the mindset of the time could produce.

On the last Sunday in August, four blind men in armor and carrying clubs entered a ring. A pig was placed in there with them. The men were told that the one who killed the pig could keep the carcass, worth several meals. The Parisian journal writer recorded the odd sight of watching the men hit each other more than they did the pig. The next weekend, the people greased a tall pole, at the top of which was a basket holding a goose and silver coins. Anyone who could climb to the top won the reward.

Countryside

Agriculture was the real king of the Middle Ages. Ninety percent of Europeans were involved in food production. The farmers did the actual labor, but the landowners had a stake too—with the buying and selling of food, they sustained their power as nobles, clerics, or military men. In exchange for having tenure of land for their own use, farmers worked three or four days a week on the fields reserved for the landowners.

Wheat, rye, barley, and oats were common crops because grain was so important across European diets. First, plows pulled by oxen were used; later, iron attachments dug and turned the soil, and finally, the invention of new restraints allowed horses to be used to cover more ground. This changed the two-crop system into a three-crop system—farmers who now had more land at their disposal could keep three fields in rotation, one for winter crops, one for spring, and one to rest.

The markets were the purview of the women. Women tended to any of the animals, like chickens and cows, that produced items that could be sold at market as well the smaller gardens.

The Political Setup

To understand how a young peasant girl living in the Middle Ages could convince the leader of one of the most powerful countries in the world to listen to the voices in her head, it's important to first understand how complicated the political situation was, how desperate the heir to the crown was, and how reasonable the word of God sounded to people with even the most earthly of responsibilities, such as governing a kingdom.

During Joan's life, there were the French and then there were how the French saw themselves: as either Armagnacs or Burgundians. At times, calling one group "French" meant risking penalty. That civil disruption would have been enough to complicate France's political climate, but the English and Scots were also sticking their noses into France's business. The **dauphin** Charles was the heir apparent to the French crown, but a lot of twists and turns had led to his claim being contested by many, even some of his countrymen. As a King's College London emeritus professor of medieval history has summarized it: "Everything was to play for."

Oppositional in so many ways, these players were united in their belief in God. More than belief, they saw his words and decisions as solid as law. And if they could get on God's side, through prayer, offering, or other devotional claims, they would be rewarded—not just in heaven but while still on earth. English King Henry V believed himself to be a soldier of God and addressed his prayers to God of Battles. The man who would be known as Charles VII took a strong affinity to St. Michael.

Opposite: The glorious Louvre behind them, French peasants work the land.

Female visionaries, who claimed to directly hear God, influenced even educated nobles.

The political world was also tangled across generations. Revenge killings could happen years after the offense. Sometimes those acts of vengeance happened within the same family. People could marry their relatives, leading to complicated branches of their name and feuds within the same family tree. It can feel complicated to the scholar of medieval history to follow all the characters, not only because of the intermarrying but also because people tended to be named after each other, leading to several individuals with the same name living at once. Names also changed with change in status—for example, the son of Charles VI was technically born the seventh Charles but he couldn't be called Charles VII until he became king.

The Complicated Leadership of France

From 1380 to his death in 1422, Charles VI was king of France, though he ruled in name only after 1392. That year he suffered a violent seizure while riding in a battle. He killed five of his own men, and from then on, his mental state fluctuated without warning from lucid to deranged.

Normally, a king physically led his army, but Charles VI was not fit to do so. The closest male relative who wasn't just an acceptable stand-in but an exemplary one was John of Burgundy, the king's cousin, who had a lot of military experience. He also was the son of the king's **regent,** Philip of Burgundy. Charles VI remained the king in name, but Philip ran the show after the king's first sign of mental illness.

In charge of the battlefield, John also expected to easily assume political power once his father died. Instead, when that happened in 1404, Charles VI's brother Louis, Duke of Orléans,

This miniature from the fifteenth century shows life around Charles VI.

challenged him for the position. For three years, they engaged in back-and-forth power plays. In 1407, frustrated by this seemingly unending cycle, John murdered Louis.

For the next two years, shielded in part by the devotion of both France's military and the citizens of Paris, John dodged verbal attacks, and likely would-be assassins' attacks too. By 1411, France was divided. On one side were the Burgundians, the supporters of John. On the other were the Armagnacs, a diversified alliance of powerful people that included not only the Orléans branch of the royal family but the nobility from the Armagnac region of France. Even after John was removed from power in 1413 and replaced with the Armagnacs, the infighting continued. And the people of France were tired of being dragged along.

The English Attack a Fractured France

This was the perfect time, from the perspective of English King Henry V, for an invasion.

As soon as Henry V's army landed in Normandy, a call to arms sounded across France. Burgundians and Armagnacs joined together to fight a more-hated enemy. They were certain that they would prevail. How could they lose, when they had a bigger army than the English, when they were less exhausted than their opponent, and when they knew the terrain? Most importantly, the French believed they had God on their side. And at that time, everything, including war, happened because of God's will.

Instead, that fall of 1415, the French lost, badly, in a battle the English would call Agincourt.

God was clearly very angry at the French.

Caught Between a Rock and a Hard Place

In hashing out what went wrong, the French, no longer feeling united and fraternal, pointed the accusatory finger at many likely offenders of God's sensibility. One rose to the top of the unenviable heap: John of Burgundy's assassination of Louis of

Orléans back in 1407 had divided the country, which made it vulnerable to outside attack.

It was decided that John must have been in cahoots with the English. John argued back that he hadn't been; two of his own brothers had been killed at Agincourt.

But John was in a difficult place because of his position in French society. He was charged with both serving and protecting France (and he still wanted to be named king) and being responsible for the economic well-being of his region, which required him to maintain a healthy trade relationship with England.

Break Down—Again

In the fall of 1416, John and Henry V agreed to a truce between England and John's northern territories of France. John did not agree, however, to support Henry in his quest to assume power over France. John still wanted that for himself. And though he hadn't been able to reach that goal by working with his countrymen, he knew that working with their sworn enemy, England, was also not the way. In fact, aligning himself to that degree with England would make him what the Armagnacs kept saying he was: a traitor.

So, John went back to maneuvering players within the government to edge himself closer to the throne and to tending his relationship with the people of France. When his political moves were foiled at every step, he resorted to publicly accusing the Armagnacs of wrongdoing. His forces began advancing on Paris.

The Armagnac regime had sent Queen Isabeau, King Charles VI's wife, into political exile because of rumors that she'd had an affair with the Duke of Orléans. This ended up helping John of

Burgundy as he edged closer to Paris; because Isabeau wanted to be freed, she welcomed him as her liberator. Now John had a direct line to the king, through the queen, but the Armagnacs also had direct favor from the king, through his son the dauphin, Charles.

Once again, France was divided.

And once again, in 1418, England attacked.

Throughout all of this, those who suffered most were the regular citizens. There were reports of French people escaping the English only to be captured by the Burgundians and then captured anew by the Armagnacs. Interestingly, the Armagnacs were always viewed as the worst, even in comparison to the invading English.

The new **pope**, Martin V, urged peace, but no one paid him any attention. The Burgundians seized Paris; the city imploded with the upheaval, pitting person against person; and the English kept advancing.

Eye for an Eye

By the summer of 1419, the main power players were John and Henry V still, as well as the dauphin, Charles, son of the still-king of France, Charles VI. Facing a heightened threat from the English, John of Burgundy arranged to have a diplomatic meeting with the dauphin.

On September 10, John and his attendants walked toward the young Charles and the latter's attendants. John knelt before the dauphin and one of Charles's attendants struck him with an ax. Armagnac troops came out of hiding to subdue John's attendants. Though Charles saw this as eye-for-eye justifiable revenge for John of Burgundy's murder of Louis of Orléans twelve long years before, not everyone agreed. The assassination of John served to finalize the divide between the Burgundians and the Armagnacs and, therefore, the entire country of France.

Just as Louis's immediate family had pressed a charming John about his death, so John's family now pressed Charles, who had his own story ready, about John's death. The difference in this go-around was that France was already divided. Recourse could only happen outside the country's borders. The next step for John's son Philip, the new Duke of Burgundy, was a big one: he could side with Charles, staying in line to become the next king of France, or he could throw his lot in with England's Henry V becoming king of France.

The New King—Sort Of

The choice was an easy one for Philip. Charles had murdered Philip's father. The people of France also ended up considering England the lesser of two evils over the Armagnacs.

Nearly five years after Agincourt, in 1420, France was fully under England's rule, and Henry V had married Charles VI's daughter Catherine. Charles VI remained king in name, but under the Treaty of Troyes, King Henry was his regent, meaning he would act as king and assume the throne upon Charles VI's death.

The Scots

This did not mean that France's Charles had given up hope of becoming king. Throughout the changeover, he gathered and maintained troops, and in January of 1421, he made an offering to St. Michael, his protector. Not actually a saint but an archangel, St. Michael also spoke to Joan. This mutual admiration for the head of God's army, the patron of soldiers, and the defender against dragons was a key commonality between Joan and Charles. With God by Charles's side, he had hope. He also placed his faith in an earthly ally, Scotland, which recognized him as the rightful heir to the throne.

The Scots hated the English as much as the French did, maybe more so. They'd been making their way to France since 1419, and by February 1421, there were thousands of Scots in France.

While Henry was back in England to introduce Catherine as the new queen—they would rule over both England and France—his brother Thomas was in charge in France. Wanting to make a name for himself, Thomas decided to knock off a faction of Armagnac rebels. He was surprised to find Scottish allies waiting with the rebels.

Buoyed by this great ambush, Charles advanced his troops. However, Henry's return to France squashed Charles's dreams. Henry brought more English soldiers with him as well as news that Catherine was pregnant with his child. Both helped to solidify his hold on France. Back and forth, this was how Charles's life went—he'd make headway in his bid for power, and then he'd lose his nerve and back down.

Surprise Deaths

Fate interceded yet again.

In August 1422, the seemingly healthy Henry took ill and, after only a few days, died. Maybe, some theorized, he'd been punished for disturbing the shrine at Meaux during a skirmish with the Armagnacs. St. Fiacre's **relics** were housed there, and his feast day had been the last day Henry had been alive.

Seven weeks later, Charles VI died. Suddenly, the result that no one had anticipated had happened: Henry and Catherine's nine-month-old baby, also named Henry, was now king of England and France.

This meant, of course, that adults scrambled to be in charge. This included Charles, who'd been attending mass two or three times daily and who felt that his destiny was clear. He renewed his offering to St. Michael and set about pushing the English out with renewed effort. His followers must have felt the renewed excitement: this was their chance to do what they couldn't have expected—return the throne to a Frenchman.

Two Capitals, Two Rulers, One Country

By 1424, France had, in essence, two capitals: Paris, where the Duke of Bedford, baby Henry's regent, lived, and Bourges, over one hundred miles south of Paris, where Charles lived. From Paris, Bedford threatened fines on anyone who called Charles king or the Armagnacs French. From Bourges, Charles countered that he was in the process of sending the English invaders into the ocean.

Yolande of Aragon: Puppetmaster

Yolande of Aragon, Duchess of Anjou, had been married to Louis of Orléans, brother of King Charles VI, whom John of Burgundy had assassinated. She was also the mother-in-law of King Charles VI's son, the Armagnac prince long in battle with the English and the Burgundians, in league with the Scots, and indebted to St. Michael. Yolande was instrumental in setting Charles up in Bourges. She also was the master of many other political designs.

In addition to all her French land holdings, she had a hereditary claim on Sicily, which was not just the island of Sicily as we know it today but also parts of mainland Italy. Her contemporaries considered her the queen of Sicily. She set her son Louis on leading his own military regiment to take the land.

She also had claim of a part of eastern France, called Bar, which her uncle ruled. Since he was a priest, however, and therefore had no children, the line of ownership would stop with him, something Yolande feared. She asked him to adopt her son René. Her purpose for this was twofold: René would eventually inherit the land owned by his uncle/adoptive father, and he also could control neighboring Lorraine through his future marriage to the Lorraine heiress, which Yolande would negotiate. By 1423, she had achieved this entire complicated plan.

Unfortunately, the only way she'd keep all this—including her third objective, her son-in-law Charles finally, officially, becoming king of France with her daughter as queen—was if England was gone from France's shores, once and for all. She began a multipronged diplomatic offensive instead of a militaristic one.

Yolande of Aragon: Believer of Female Visionaries

Yolande was also open to the idea of God speaking through women. Years before, her mother-in-law had told her of a peasant woman who'd been healed of a previously incurable illness by visiting a sacred grave and who then started receiving messages from God. Yolande's mother-in-law took notice and wholly believed the woman.

Yolande took heed of her mother-in-law's example so that when she met another female visionary, in 1400, she listened to her. The woman so proved her abilities to Yolande that Yolande stood as a witness in the woman's canonization hearing to be named as a saint. So, not only was Yolande open to diplomacy among men but she was also interested in God's plan.

Yolande of Aragon was the stepmother of Charles VII.

In 2003, people gathered in St. Peter's Square before the Vatican.

THE SMALLEST COUNTRY, HEADQUARTERS OF CHRISTIANITY'S LARGEST DENOMINATION

Though the Catholic institutions, both physical and spiritual, within its walls date to well before Joan of Arc's time, the Vatican City State is not even one hundred years old. It was founded in 1929 following the signing of the Lateran Pacts between the **Holy See** and Italy.

The Vatican is the headquarters of the Roman Catholic Church and the home of the church's leader, the pope. It's also an independent, sovereign, nation—the tiniest in the world! Only about eight hundred people call it home, and about half of those don't live there full-time because their jobs, often in diplomatic relations, require them to work so closely with other countries that they live in those countries. The walled Vatican City is about one hundred acres large. It is the most visited place in the world, per capita, with more than five million visitors each year.

St. Peter's **Basilica**, named for St. Peter, around whose tomb the church was constructed, is the country's focal point. Peter was head of the **apostles** and the first **bishop** of Rome. The basilica was built in the fourth century and rebuilt, with a dome designed by Michelangelo, in the sixteenth century. From its foundation in St. Peter's Square to the top of the spire on that dome, the basilica is around forty stories tall. Visitors can reach the top of the dome by climbing 551 steps. As much of a site for prayer and worship as it is, St. Peter's is also considered a great cultural institution, housing many impressive works of art, including the **frescoes** of Michelangelo in the Sistine Chapel. The paintings, depicting scenes from the Book of Genesis, cover 8,200 square feet.

When he is in town, the pope blesses the crowd in the square from a window in the basilica on Sundays at noon. He lives at the Palace of the Vatican, as popes have since 1377.

CHAPTER TWO

The Life *of* Joan *of* Arc

W hen one thinks of Joan, one most often imagines a serious religious devotee, a serious soldier of the French monarchy, maybe even a serious laborer on her family's farm before she left home to meet her military destiny. All of that is true, but it's also important to remember that she was just nineteen when she was executed, and only fourteen when she arranged her first meeting with the heir to the French crown, the dauphin Charles. Childhood and adolescence didn't mean then what they do today, but still, even with the responsibilities Joan had to bear, she was a young person. She could be mature only to a degree. Indeed, Joan herself talked of her time playing under a "fairy tree," a giant beech near a stream that the townspeople believed was made of healing waters. Girls were known to hang garlands of flowers from its branches and dance in its shade.

Opposite: Joan of Arc listens to God outside her childhood home.

What's in a Name?

Joan was born Jehanne d'Arc, Jehanne Tarc or Jehanne Darc, Jehanne Romée, or Jehanne de Vouthon. Jehanne sounds a bit like Joan—at least to English speakers' ears, which is how she has come to be referred to as that. Her family name is a bit more of a mystery.

D'Arc was the last name of her father, Jacques, Joan said during her trial; Tarc and Darc are forms of d'Arc. Some believe that Romée was the surname of her mother, Isabelle, but Romée is less of a last name as we think of them today and more of designation for a person who's made a religious **pilgrimage**. So, it's possible that other scholars are correct and that Joan's mother went by the last name of de Vouthon.

Scholars are uncertain about her name for several reasons. In medieval France, last names weren't used consistently or frequently. When Joan testified early in her trial that she didn't know her last name, she might have been speaking sincerely. Later in the trial, when she shared her parents' names, she said that in her town, girls often took their mothers' last names.

As a girl, Joan answered to Jehanette. During her trial, she called herself Jehanne la Pucelle, Joan the Maid. By doing this, she emphasized her youthful innocence and her servitude, both of which were important in her establishing the parallel between herself and her own hero, the Virgin Mary: both were pure and in complete service to God.

Joan's Family

Joan was born in 1412 in Domrémy, a village in Bar in northeastern France, which Yolande of Aragon owned and

This illustration by Paul de Semant shows Joan after the king's coronation.

her uncle, and then her son, administered. The house in which she was born still exists, now as a museum. Joan's father worked as a farmer, and her devout Catholic mother raised the children and helped with the farm's animals and gardens. Joan had four siblings, brothers Jacquemin, Jean, and Pierre, and sister Catherine.

Her father was born around 1375, her mother around 1385. Isabelle was from near Domrémy, which is why they settled there. Though Jacques was a farmer, documents point to him having power in his community, maybe even a degree of wealth. He bought the Chateau de L'Ile in 1419 and was described in a document dated 1423 as holding a position in town that was somewhere between mayor and provost, and he was responsible for collecting taxes.

Two of Joan's brothers, Pierre, born in 1408, and Jean, born in 1409, along with their mother, were at Joan's nullification trial to clear her name after her death. Joan's brother Jacquemin was born in 1402 and died in 1450. He was married to Catherine Corviset. Joan's sister Catherine was born in 1413 and went on to marry a man named Colin, who was the son of the mayor of Greux, a town a few hundred yards from Domrémy. She died when she was sixteen years old, in childbirth, right before Joan left to serve the dauphin Charles. That Joan left home at such a sad time for her family shows how important her work was to her.

It also shows that Joan wasn't always that close with her family. She didn't tell them about the voices she heard or the commands they gave her to help the dauphin. Her father wished Joan would just get married and live a normal life—in fact, he arranged a marriage for her. Joan wanted nothing to do with that. When she was sixteen years old, she argued before the court in the town of Toul to have her father's marriage promise overturned. She succeeded.

Joan's Pastimes

With no school to attend and living far from the bustle of a city, Joan stayed close to home for her first fourteen years, until she traveled to talk to Charles about voices in her head. Imagine it:

Joan's first experience outside her hometown was a meeting with a prince.

Joan's mother taught her about God. From Isabelle's last name, a marker of being a pilgrim, we can assume she made a pilgrimage to Rome, which was a huge undertaking in that day. Throughout Domrémy, Joan was known to be pious and devout. The warden of the church adjacent to Joan's childhood home certainly was aware of this: he was the recipient of her rare cross words anytime he was late ringing the church bells. She herself was never late to mass.

Though that church has changed a lot since Joan's time, its statue of St. Margaret, before which Joan knelt and prayed, remains. She also used to drop to her knees in the field to pray at the end of each workday. She went to confession daily, sometimes more than once a day.

Joan was also known for her work around her family's farm, caring for the family's herd of cattle, as a woman might, but also participating in heavy labor. Joan had a sturdy physical stature and "a virile [man-like] bearing," which was enhanced by her work. As her muscles grew, so did her clout around town. In addition to her surprising strength, she was also known for having more traditional female traits: she had "a pretty, woman's voice"; she "readily shed[s] copious tears"; and she had "a cheerful face." In other words, she probably looked like a well-rounded teenager.

Joan was also known for being skillful at making and mending clothes. At her trial in Rouen, she said, "I fear no woman in Rouen at sewing and spinning." On trial for life, her core beliefs challenged with charges of serious crimes, she was still confident.

The First Voice

As France's government heaved and splintered again, with Henry V's and Charles VI's deaths, Joan of Arc's little corner of the country also began to crack.

In 1425, the English and Burgundians charged through Joan's town, releasing cattle and burning property. In Joan's time, France was a divided country of tangled allegiances. For the common person, that meant living in what must have sometimes felt like lawless conditions. Growing up in Domrémy, Joan had learned to fear the Burgundians. Marching across her homeland in northern France, they presented as a marauding army even though they were, until a year before her birth, just her countrymen. Joan's town supported the dauphin Charles—traditionally, Domrémy was in a unique region, ruled not by a noble as most regions were, but directly by the king. That may at least in part explain why they stuck with the French royal line even while neighboring regions sided with the Burgundians.

There had long been occasional violent skirmishes in this new borderland. Joan said at her trial that she grew up watching as "children literally fought children." Soon after, at thirteen years old, Joan started hearing voices.

One day while Joan was working in her father's garden, she heard something, a voice coming from the right of her, someone saying something in French. She looked up and had to shield her eyes against a brilliant white light.

The entire event shook her very being.

As her heart quieted, she considered what she'd heard. It had been a female voice, telling her to be pious in life. But neither her sister nor her mother, nor any friends or neighbors were nearby.

Opposite: In Lucien Lantier's 1920 painting, Joan of Arc listens to Saints Catherine, Margaret, and Michael, her voices from God.

That was but the first of the voices. During an interrogation on February 22, 1431, Joan said she heard the voices "two or three times a week," and on March 1, she said, "There is never a day that I do not hear them [the voices]." On March 12, she said the voices even disturbed her rest: "I was asleep: the Voice woke me … It awoke me without touching me."

Eventually, Joan became used to them, welcomed them, sometimes even beckoned them to her. The church bells sometimes heralded them making an appearance—now Joan had a reason besides respectful punctuality to want the warden to ring the church bells on time. Noise or the presence of other people kept the voices at bay—that may have been why, as Joan grew used to her visitors, she increasingly isolated herself.

Joan identified spirits who visited her as Saints Catherine, Margaret, and Michael. He appeared as a good-looking gentleman, and the women appeared as floating faces, though Joan said that she "embraced" them once, and they smelled wonderful. When questioned at her trial about how she interacted with just faces, she replied, "I leave that to God." Her answer as to why an English saint such as Margaret would speak French was handled just as deftly: "Why would she speak English when she is not on the English side?"

During her trial, she testified that the first messages from the angels and saints were that she live a godly life, attending church and living piously.

Then they told her to cut her long hair into the pageboy style common among French knights.

Joan's First Attempt to Meet the Dauphin

In 1428, Joan visited the Armagnac military outpost closest to her, the garrison at the town of Vaucouleurs, ten miles north of

Joan's hometown of Domrémy. The captain there heard what the sixteen-year-old had to say, but ultimately he sent her away, rejecting her request to be taken to meet Charles. Later, he would say he thought her family needed to slap her out of her delusions.

Joan's Successful Attempt to Meet the Dauphin

Undaunted, Joan returned at the end of the year, and this time her effort was rewarded. The Duke of Lorraine, the father-in-law of Yolande's son René, had decided to hear Joan out. As Yolande had learned to believe female visionaries from her mother-in-law, this man had also learned from direct and indirect experience—perhaps including Yolande's influence on him via Rene. The Armagnac captain next decided to allow Joan to go to Charles, at Chinon.

Gossip had spread about this strange visitor, and the Vaucouleurs townspeople wanted to help her. She was wearing a rough red dress, no good for long-distance traveling, so they outfitted Joan with a man's wardrobe—black and gray hat, tunic, doublet, hose, breeches—and gave her a horse. Joan welcomed these gifts because the voices had told her to dress as a man.

On February 13, 1429, Joan and the men assigned to accompany her as support and protection—and perhaps also to keep an eye on this strange creature—left Vaucouleurs for Chinon. Historians have estimated the rate of speed by horse in medieval times as anywhere from fifteen miles in a day, by a household traveling together, to sixty miles a day, by a messenger. It took Joan's small band ten tense days to cover two hundred seventy miles, some of it controlled by the Burgundians. They arrived on February 23, 1429.

A royal messenger accompanied them, which meant that the court and Yolande knew Joan was coming. This was lucky: God's word may have gotten Joan in the door, but Yolande taking the teenage girl dressed in men's clothing immediately under her wing allowed Joan to meet Charles.

Joan told him that God's gift for him was not just instructions on how to secure his place as king but her, Joan, God's conduit and Charles's willing soldier. Specifically, she wanted to drive the English from France and lead Charles from Chinon to Reims for **coronation**.

The Pros and Cons of Joan

Joan had a lot going for her: She had the people and the military at Vaucouleurs on her side. She had not only a compelling message for a court and a citizenry desperate for good news, but also an influential friend in Yolande. She was capturing the imagination of the people of Chinon. And, of course, finally, she'd had an in-person meeting with the dauphin.

She also had a lot not in her favor. Satan could speak to people as readily as God could, and Charles was not certain that a holy hand guided this young visitor. The common belief at the time was that women were more susceptible than men to demonic deception. Her boastfulness—that she should lead him to victory against the English—was more befitting the devil than a lady. In addition to being a vulnerable female, Joan was young, inexperienced, and uneducated. She also wore suspicious clothing. Charles appreciated that it had helped her ride her horse unencumbered and that the oversize outfit was held on her body with lots of knotted ropes, offering some protection against sexual assault as she traveled without a female chaperone. Still, he felt compelled to follow God's word, and the Bible's book of Deuteronomy clearly stated that a woman in men's clothing was "an abomination."

Opposite: Published in a 1901 history book on England, this image shows Joan at Charles VII's court in 1429.

Charles decided to put Joan of Arc through a battery of tests to check the validity of her story.

The Testing of Joan

First, Charles ordered two women to confirm Joan's physical purity. Then he sent her on another long journey, forty miles south to Poitiers, where theologians questioned her about her life and purpose. At the end of three weeks, though they remained cautious, the experts could not deny that her answers consistently displayed righteousness and goodness. They had received no negative responses from God during all their prayers about Joan.

Orléans became the tipping point. When the theologians protested that the city, under English control for six months now, physically blocked the path to Reims, making Joan's plan to lead an impossibility, Joan said, fine, she'd take care of Orléans first.

This seemed like a suitable practical test for Joan—the English company that held Orléans was small in number, and even if Joan lost, it wouldn't be an embarrassingly huge defeat for Charles. She wouldn't lose the Armagnacs a city, they just wouldn't regain it.

The experts reported their conclusions in the "Poitiers Conclusions." They wrote, "Given his own needs and those of his kingdom, and considering the continual prayers of his poor people to God and to all others who love peace and justice, the king should neither reject nor resist the Maid."

Joan Commands an Army

Charles ordered her virginity to be confirmed once more—Yolande performed the examination herself this time—and then she was given her major opportunity.

Joan's first task was to write a letter to England. She wanted to offer them one last chance to withdraw from Orléans. She also wanted to be clear with them that if they didn't stand down, she—the Maid, as she called herself for the first time—would rain terror down on them, with God by her side. The following is part of the letter she dictated on March 22, as shared in Lee Wind's book *The Queer History Project*. Her devotion to God's demands as well as his forgiveness is obvious in her own strong words.

Depart in God's name for your own country. If you do not, wait for word from the Maid, who will come see you shortly, to your great dismay. King of England, if you refuse this, I am a captain of war, and wherever I find your men in France, I will force them to leave, whether they wish to or not. If they refuse to obey, I will have them all killed. I am sent by God, the King of Heaven, to chase you one and all from France. If they obey, I shall have mercy on them. Do not think otherwise, for you shall never rule the kingdom of France, by God the King of Heaven, holy Mary's son, but Charles the true heir will rule it. God wills it, and has revealed it to him through the Maid … If you refuse to believe these tidings from God and the Maid, when we find you, we shall strike you and make a greater uproar than France has heard for a thousand years, if you fail to do right by us. And know full well that the King of Heaven will send the Maid more strength than you could muster in all your assaults against her and her good men-at-arms … The Maid prays and requests you not to destroy yourselves. If you do right, you can still come join her company, where the French will perform the finest action ever seen in Christian lands. Answer, if you wish to make peace in the city of Orléans. If you do not, prepare yourselves soon for a great loss.

Joan holds her banner in this fifteen-century miniature that imagines what she looked like.

JOAN OF ARC: A HISTORY

Reviewers widely praised historian Helen Castor's *Joan of Arc: A History* when it was published in 2015, and this book owes a debt to Castor's work. After six centuries of talk about the military leader, it can be hard to find something new to say. Castor succeeded in adding a useful book to the Joan of Arc library by explaining the culture and politics that supported Joan's rise. Her book's *New York Times* review called *Joan of Arc: A History* important because it does what so many books don't do: set Joan as a human being.

Born in 1968, Castor is a London historian of the medieval period. She has lectured in history at Cambridge University and directed the history department at Sidney Sussex College. She's presented history programs on British television and radio, including a three-part television program on her 2010 book *She-Wolves: The Women Who Ruled England Before Elizabeth.* She was inspired to write her first book about women in political power by thinking about when British King Edward VI lay dying at age fifteen in July 1553. "That moment must have been terrifying for the men standing around Edward's deathbed," she said in an interview with HistoryToday.com. In their minds—and in their hearts—women could not and should not be in positions of power, yet there were no males left in the royal Tudor family line. As soon as the boy died, a female would take his place in leading the British empire. This, Castor realized, was not the first time women in England assumed positions of power or came close to it. *She-Wolves* studies Empress Matilda (1102–1167), Eleanor of Aquitaine (around 1122–1204), Isabella of France (circa 1295–1358), and Margaret of Anjou (1430–1482).

Jehanne

CHAPTER THREE

Waging War

Joan never killed anyone. When she charged forward in battle, she raised a banner showing two angels and God, holding the world in his hand, that unfurled in her wake.

But don't think for a moment that she wasn't the military hero she is remembered as. She was her soldiers' inspiration, never leaving their side. She was their strategist too, both directing the troops and proposing diplomatic alternatives. And though Joan was never on the literal front line, she put herself on the line, backing up her words with actions. She was wounded at least three times, once by arrow, once by rock, and once by crossbow bolt.

Ceremony

Charles welcomed his new military leader back to Chinon with grand ceremony. The experts who interrogated Joan at Charles's behest might have feared the embarrassment of a public failure, but the French royal family were nothing if not lovers of pomp.

Opposite: Joan of Arc's signature, from a March 16, 1430 letter, is a rare look at her handwriting.

Over the course of the Hundred Years' War, the poignancy of metaphor guided where they scheduled diplomatic negotiations, and they'd celebrated wins by replacing the city's water reserves with wine. And so Joan was presented one by one with leaders pretending to be Charles until she correctly uncovered the actual dauphin.

Joan was a willing participant in the fanfare, requesting Charles's men go to Sainte-Catherine-de-Fierbois to fetch a hidden sword from the church of the patron saint of virgins, Catherine. Everyone was amazed when a sword was found hidden behind the altar. "This sword was in the earth, all rusty, and there were upon it five crosses," Joan said during her trial, when asked how she'd known a sword would be there, "and I knew it by my voices."

The king's secretaries added to the mysticism. They searched the royal archives for indication that Joan herself had been prophesized and declared they'd found not one but two mentions, one of a "maid bearing flowers," another in which a "virgin ascends the backs of archers."

Preparing for Battle

Practical matters were also attended to. Copies of the "Poitiers Conclusions" were distributed across the land, and rumors permeated even Orléans of, historian Helen Castor wrote, "a miraculous maid who was coming to save them." The king's armorer handmade Joan's suit of armor, and for three weeks, she practiced walking and riding a horse while wearing the strange weight of it. A squire, two pages, and a chaplain were all assigned to her, and the men who would ride in her company got used to the idea of being led by a teenage girl—this unique girl who forced them to go to confession before they could join her ranks.

The Battle of Orléans

On April 21, Joan met her men and the company's supplies in Blois, thirty-five miles from Chinon, and the letter that she'd dictated to the English a month before was sent on to Orléans. Though the adrenaline running through the men's bodies must have been practically crackling, so anxious were they to do what they had been trained to do, Joan reminded them firmly that if the English did take her up on her offer to stand down, the French were not to exact revenge but let the enemy retreat in peace. She slept in her suit of armor her last night at Blois, April 25, 1429.

Joan's Sharp Tongue

Joan wasn't scared to speak her mind to men sometimes twice her age and with a lot more experience. She'd always had confidence, but she displayed a new level of brazenness once placed in charge. She'd rejected society's and her family's expectations that she marry in favor of a religious servitude that struck even her contemporaries as a bit extreme. She'd dealt with, all by herself, the voices in her head. And she'd arranged meetings with military and royal leaders. Through it all, she'd been sweet-tempered, but with human lives and the future of her country on the line—not to mention God's edict—she didn't hide behind an accommodating smile. If a soldier crossed her, whether by ignoring her suggestions for battle or by swearing or skipping mass, she gave him a piece of her mind. Once, she even tried to slap a Scottish ally when she found out he'd stolen some meat. She had zero patience when prostitutes came calling at her men's camp, drawing her sword on them. When she was frustrated at the situation they were in, she lashed out at the nobility that had put them there, calling them spineless when it came to the English.

First Sighting of Orléans

On April 26, Joan's company marched out of the forest to the south of the Loire River and got their first look at Orléans, a city the French did not want to lose because of its location along this major waterway.

And the English, who of course knew from Joan's letter that the French were coming, got their first sight of the Armagnacs. Priests carrying a banner of the crucifixion and singing "Come, Holy Spirit" led the men and the carts of provisions for the citizens of Orléans, and then came the Maid. The English were relatively few in number and hungry after the long winter, but they doubted it would take much to subdue what the Armagnacs sent their way.

Just as the French had met Joan with skepticism, so too did the English from their position in the **fortified** tower called Tourelles. They were not going to back down from this pompous, mad, unladylike teenage witch. They hurled insults at her; whether their blasphemy toward God or their disrespect toward her hurt her more, it was said that their words filled her with rage. Throughout the week and a half of on-off (mostly off) fighting that it took the Armagnacs to defeat the English at Orléans, the enemy camps would be so close to each other that each could hear the other's words: mockery from the English directed at

Joan, and from Joan, frustration at her enemy's insolence as well as unwavering faith in God displayed in confessions and mass.

Unfortunately, what happened after Joan's arrival at Orléans was anything but the glorious battle Joan must have imagined. Against her wishes, her priests and most of her men stayed by the Loire. Joan believed God would provide, but the military commanders believed it was up to France to provide, and it made no sense to them to bring food to the hungry people of Orléans along with more people to feed. While Joan's less impressive group advanced, the Orleanais staged a raid on the **bastille** in order to distract the English. It worked: Joan, her company, and the provisions slipped inside without attack by the English.

If only Joan could have seen how she looked to the people of Orléans as she rode among them on her regal white horse. In her armor, she glowed in the light from their torches. They cheered for her and strained to touch any part of her. But all Joan could see was her thwarted plan—squashed by the people under her own command! And still England mocked her from the nearby tower.

Holding Pattern

Joan wrote again to the English, demanding they stand down. Now that they'd seen exactly what Joan was all about, their reply was bolder than their last: one of the English in command, Lord Talbot, called her a trollop and then threatened to burn her at the stake. Did Joan roar in frustration at this response, kick the ground, or throw a stone at the wall? She did take off running for the fortifications protecting the city, climbed them, and screamed at the English that they should surrender to God. This just made them laugh harder, the voice belonging to Captain Sir William Glasdale raising above the others.

One of Joan's commanders saw how much hope she gave the Orléanians. He also believed Joan might be their savior. What he knew for sure was that if she wasn't allowed to act, they'd never know her truth. The next day, he rode out to retrieve the rest of Joan's army.

While he was gone, Joan made a show of checking out the geography of the area. The people rewarded her for it, gushing whenever she circled back to them and organizing a procession in her honor.

The Attack

On May 4, 1429, the rest of the soldiers returned, and the whole group immediately staged their first attack, on the bastille on the eastern side of the city. The battle took three hours. Though she carried no weapon, Joan rode her horse among the men, urging them to glory.

Over the next six months, the sounds, sights, smells of battle—tastes too, as mud flew in the mouth or the stench became so potent as to carry a taste—would become familiar to Joan. Layered within the boom of the cannon and shrieks of the **artillery** were sounds of injured men and horses in agony. If there was a muddy moat, the Armagnac soldiers splashed into it, dragging wood with them to build a rough path to the scalable walls. Joan was always the first into the moat.

That night of May 4, after her first battle, the reality of war hit her hard. No longer feeling righteous or raring to go, she stayed quiet over her barely touched dinner, massaging her aching muscles. She dictated another letter to the English. Perhaps not willing to risk another messenger—the herald who delivered her first letter was taken prisoner—or perhaps because she did remain incensed, albeit more introspectively now, she attached it to an arrow and ordered it shot to the English. She didn't need to wait long for their reply—all of Orléans heard Captain Glasdale's cry of "News from the Armagnac whore!"

The Advancement

On May 6, after confession and mass, Joan and her men edged closer to where the English were holed up in Tourelles. The day was long and bloody on both sides, but the French prevailed. All that was left was the tower.

It was during the May 7 battle for Tourelles that an arrow pierced Joan's skin between her neck and shoulder. The reaction of Joan's soldiers to her injury showed that they hadn't fallen under the taunting spell of the English, nor had they lost faith in the teenager who had yet to draw her sword. They were so shaken to see their Maid bleeding that the commander nearly ordered a retreat. Realizing this, Joan quickly stood and lifted her banner high in the air. A cry went up from the soldiers, and they surged forward once again.

A while later, a twist of a fate, divine or otherwise, caused English Captain Glasdale to slip from his perch high up in the tower and fall into the Loire River rushing past. When he did not reappear, his men lost their ability to function.

That night, Joan went to bed while the Orléanians celebrated, ringing the church bells and asking the town's patron saints of Aignan and Euverte to bless the Maid. She, and her men, had more work to do come the morning. Armagnac sentries reported that the English stationed a little farther out were preparing to march on Orléans.

William Etty's painting, more than three hundred years after her death, shows the Maid riding from Orléans.

Waiting

On May 8, the French rode out to meet the English, pulling up short under Joan's command that they were to go on the defensive, not the offensive. They should fight only if the enemy attacked first.

They waited.

Finally, the order to retreat rose from the English command. Joan had been right to restrain her men. The English had also been told not to fight unless they were attacked, and since the past few days had weakened them, they chose to withdraw rather than risk losing more soldiers.

Joan mania spread immediately, not surprisingly within Orléans but also as far away as Rome, where a bishop amended his brief history of the world to include her. On May 13, Charles thanked Joan in person when she met up with him. Her work was not yet done, though, and she didn't linger in his praise. She urged him to go to Reims as soon as possible for the coronation. Unfortunately, she wouldn't be able to lead him there for another month—it would take that long for new troops to be readied to clear the path to Reims of English outposts.

Battle at Jargeau

On June 11, 1429, Joan and her new band of men readied for the battle at Jargeau. Again, Joan tried diplomacy before bloodshed, sending a message to the English. And again they refused, though they didn't mock her this time. The military commanders on the French side hadn't expected the English to take the offer. The city was heavily fortified, and word was that reinforcements were on their way.

The French were anxious now and suggested to Joan that they wait or maybe meet the reinforcements and battle them first, before they reached Jargeau. The scorn for Joan was gone from the English and so was the disregard for Joan's orders from the French. When she said no, they should attack Jargeau right then, they listened. Almost immediately, a rock thrown by an English soldier struck Joan on her head, but her rising to her feet again inspired her men, and after four hours, the city was almost won back. The city became theirs when the French captured the Earl of Suffolk, who knighted his captor so that he could surrender to someone he considered honorable.

Battle at Meung

Meung, ten miles away, was next. By then, the English reinforcements that the French had feared at Jargeau were close. In this instance, both diplomacy and warfare worked. Joan and her commanders convinced the opposing commander, Richemont, from Bourges to join them, and together they took down the English forces. As Castor wrote, Richemont had not been seen for months. The only thing that had changed in the war was the involvement of this mythical Maid, and "if God were to grant famous victories against the English, he wanted a share of the glory."

The Importance of Reims

The June 18 Battle of Patay was Joan's final challenge and marked the end of a campaign that had taken only seven weeks to complete. Joan turned her attention to Reims. Charles didn't have to go through the symbolic coronation or do so only in that city.

He could be king without the coronation. In fact, many in court urged him to forget about it and focus on the English remaining in their country, such as those threatening the important region of Normandy.

But Reims was important to Joan. The ceremony was God's sanctioning of Charles's kingship. The sacred oil of Clovis was there. Clovis I is considered the first king of France, though he ruled over a place not yet called France. He lived from 466 to 511 CE and united the Frankish tribes under his one rule. He is also considered the reason Catholicism is popularly practiced in France still today. The Holy Ampulla, containing the oil supposedly in Clovis's baptism, was found right before Louis VII's coronation in 1131. From then until French revolutionaries smashed the vial in 1793, all but three of France's kings were anointed at Reims Cathedral with this holy oil that bound them in service in God's name. So, Joan insisted they focus on Reims. Not only had God said, but Joan said.

Gender Bending

By the time Joan and her men had secured Charles's route to Reims, she was, by her own admission, a soldier. When she took off her armor at night, she put on men's clothes. The Duke of Orléans sent her a present upon her freeing of his people: a robe and short jacket in the finest of fabrics of brilliant crimson and deep green, the colors of the house of Orléans. The men's garments were tailored for her feminine body.

She acted like a man too, swilling wine and sending gifts to the grandmother of the nobleman, Guy de Laval, who'd been enthralled with her since the battle of Orléans, though she had no interest in him beyond friendship.

Joan of Arc was not shy in front of a crowd.

Asked during her trial whether she had been commanded to wear men's clothing, she said that she did so not at any soldier's command but at the word of God through his saints and angels, who spoke to her. "If he commanded me to put on something else, I would do it, since this would be by God's command." The clothing was a small matter to her, one of the least important. She was fighting for God and country—what did it matter what she wore?

Journeying to Reims

For the first time in years, enrollment in the Armagnac military was up. On June 29, 1429, Charles led an army of thousands toward Reims. Taking Joan's idea, he sent letters ahead, telling the English that if they laid down their arms, all would be forgiven.

The town of Troyes still believed in their pledge of allegiance to Henry V, who had, after all, lawfully taken the crown. Though he was dead, that didn't mean they should switch to his enemy Charles. A friar named Brother Richard had been preaching in Paris and Troyes since April about the coming of the Antichrist, and the people of Troyes were fairly certain that he meant Joan of Arc.

Amazingly, Brother Richard met with Joan and returned to his people exclaiming over how impressed he'd been by the young woman. The town's elders decided that the man they'd been following so faithfully up until that point must be a sorcerer. They prepared to fight to the death to defend their dead king Henry, but when days passed and reinforcements never arrived, the elders felt stuck.

Charles was frozen outside the gates in deciding how to proceed, and the town was frozen inside them. Joan was completely befuddled. God had said to go this way. She didn't understand her king's and her army's hesitancy. The military commanders finally acquiesced, since they had already come this far, and since they did hate to doubt Joan after all her past successes. While the army prepared its assault, Joan rode forward, and the town's resolve crumbled.

More useful than Charles's letters, the elders of Troyes sent word to Reims that they strongly urged that city to accept Charles as king; next, Châlons, twenty-five miles outside of Reims, sent a similar letter. By the time Charles, Joan, and the men had closed that distance by half, representatives from Reims had met them in peace.

The Coronation

On the evening of July 16, 1429, Joan and her king rode through the gates of Reims. At 9:00 the next morning, he stepped into the town's cathedral. Joan stood next to him throughout the coronation, wearing her armor and carrying her banner. Even Joan's family was in attendance, their trip paid for by the king. She cried after he became Charles VII, feeling a huge weight finally lifting from her. "Noble king," she said, "God's will is done."

More Work to Be Done

Reality set in again. God had told Joan to get Charles to coronation and to rid France of the English. The first task was complete, but the second was not, and God had not given her details on how to accomplish this.

Joan suddenly needed to make the decision she felt was best, without God's guidance. It was the first time she had faced such a dilemma.

Joan wrote not once but twice to the Duke of Burgundy. She knew that the only way for France to be totally rid of England's

presence and for France to truly be made whole again would be if the Duke of Burgundy would stand by the new Armagnac king's side. In her second letter, she said, "Joan the Maid calls upon you by the king of heaven … that you and the king of France should make a good and lasting peace."

King Charles VII felt that releasing Paris from the English-Burgundian hold was the crucial next step. He and the duke struck a deal in which the duke had to release Paris within two weeks. That seemed to satisfy a lot of people in court, including, of course, the king.

Joan felt pulled in one direction by her fidelity to Charles and tugged in the other direction by her suspicion that Burgundy would never in actuality submit to the king. She also was uncertain that Paris was the right next step. Certainly, if that major city transferred to Charles, the English would, for all intents and purposes, lose everything. But she was tasked by God to free France of the English, not specifically to free Paris. Most distressing, she had no one to discuss this with. She was being left out of policy and strategy talks among the king's military commanders. They seemed to have decided she wasn't an overall great leader but a momentarily great one—and that "the moment of miracles had passed."

On August 7, 1429, just a couple days into the countdown to Burgundy's freeing of Paris, the duke did indeed change his mind about the truce. Yet again, revenge years in the making surprised everyone and changed everything. The Duke of Bedford, brother of the late Henry V, craftily reminded the Duke of Burgundy about John of Burgundy's assassination at Charles's hand ten years before. He also told the Parisians about Brother Richard's about-face. This bothered them because they'd trusted the friar for a long

Opposite: Joan of Arc celebrates King Charles VII's coronation in 1429, as painted by Jules Eugene Lenepveu in 1886–1890.

time. They were confused by his quick turn to side with Joan and the Armagnacs. At the leadership and the citizenry levels, Paris dug in its heels against the court of Charles VII.

Back to War

On August 14, Joan found herself back on the battlefield again, this time outside of Montepilloy, north of Paris. Each side tried to tempt the other into making the first move, but neither took the other's bait. Again, Joan ended up riding right up to the enemy line, yelling at them to attack. So continued this part of the war for another two weeks; basically, not much was happening.

Finally, in September, Joan and her company pushed forward to Paris. As they expected, the city had been fortified to the hilt, but Joan hadn't imagined its reality: thick walls with imperceptible slits through which arrows could be shot; places for big guns to rest; protected boulevards to the six gates; and a moat around the entire city.

On September 8, they rode to the gate that led to the palace of the Louvre. By nightfall, having made no headway to breach the walls, Joan yelled for the English to consider God and surrender. Insults rained down upon her, and then so did a bolt shot from a crossbow. From this injury she could not rise, as she could from her wounds at Orléans and Jargeau, but she kept screaming for her men to march onward. When the signal to retreat was given, the men had to drag her back in retreat.

Within days, Burgundian scholars were calling the retreat a sure sign that Joan was working on behalf of the devil. Or maybe the problem was that she was so bloodthirsty—God didn't want war but peace. He certainly did not want war on Mary's feast day, September 8, when Joan had attacked Paris. Never mind that when men were in charge, the entire Hundred Years' War was considered a result of God's desires.

Still, Joan persisted. In late October, healed from her physical wounds but spiritually weary, she urged her men forward to take Saint-Pierre. On November 4, the town fell. The momentum was slowly starting again, and Joan turned toward the next little town, La Charité. For the first time in all her letter writing, on November 9, she signed her own name to the letter she had dictated to the people of Reims, asking for supplies. She did not gush about the glory of God in this letter; she didn't even begin it, as had been her custom, with Jesus's name.

Desperation

Orléans had fallen in four days, but La Charité hadn't fallen after four weeks. The troops withdrew, relieved because they were starving and cold and denied more provisions from the French government. Joan wandered about for a while, finally holing up in the castle in Sully. She seemed to have no clout and no purpose. The daughter of the painter who had designed her first banner was getting married and asked if the government might help with a little of the expense, in Joan's name. They responded that they could not. Worse than that, Joan continued to receive messages of growing urgency from the people of Reims, who were fearful of what appeared to be unstable times yet again. They did not want to get recaptured. Joan responded to their pleas with comforting words and promises that she would come if they needed her, but she couldn't have believed that. Once "the court … no longer knew what to do with" Joan, Castor wrote, even she realized that "a woman on a battlefield became an alarming liability."

Interestingly, it was in this moment that Charles VII bestowed nobility on Joan, as well as her family. The raise in status hardly mattered to the despondent Joan—she answered to God, not the king.

At the end of March 1430, another letter from Joan showed just how frantic she was starting to feel about her stagnant situation. She wrote to people outside the Hundred Years' War, about a matter not of her concern at all. To the Hussites fighting in Bohemia, she wrote a version of the letter she'd repeatedly sent the English: "Reports and widespread rumors have been reaching me, Joan the Maid, that you have turned from being true Christians … Unless I hear that you have mended your ways, I may well abandon the English and march against you … and strip you of either your heresy or your lives." The Hussites surely couldn't care less what this person said, busy as they were in the practicalities of their own war. But still Joan wrote and sent her letter, like a slightly nosy neighbor.

Capture

Thankfully, by the end of the month, Joan was riding again. She and her men roamed around a twenty-five-mile radius from Paris, skirmishing with the English as they encountered them. On May 6, a letter from Charles admitted that the Duke of Burgundy was beyond hope—he still sided with England, and the Armagnacs would have to fight.

Toward the end of May, Joan led her men to take the town of Compiègne. She expected the entirety of the enemy to be before her, but another division surprised her by stepping out of hiding only once she'd been separated from her men.

She screamed to her men that God was with them until the enemy reached her and she was dragged from her horse. She formally submitted to the Burgundians and was taken, amid gawkers delighted to see the Maid proved a false prophet, to a castle at Beaulieu-les-Fontaines seventeen miles away.

King Charles did not reach out to pay a ransom on her; in fact, he'd found another messenger from heaven, a shepherd boy who suggested that Joan had done as she wanted, not as God wanted. More interested in money than a prisoner in his bid to establish Burgundy as its own independent nation, the Duke of Burgundy negotiated with the English to take Joan. The English king, another Henry, only eight years old, ordered that Joan be bought from the Burgundians.

While her life was being negotiated, Joan tried to escape her captors by squeezing between her cell's floorboards. They moved her to a higher security castle, the fortress of Beaurevoir thirty miles away. That didn't step Joan from trying again to escape. She jumped from the window of her tower prison. At her trial, she would admit that the voices had counseled her not to jump, but in a surprising break with God's will, she had decided she would, wishing her soul to be in God's hands rather than in those of the English. She did not die from her fall, nor could she scramble away. Again, she was beaten, physically and spiritually.

In November, she was handed over to the English. On January 3, 1431, it was announced that she would be put on trial, judged by the Catholic Church, but returned each night not to a church prison with nuns to guard her but to military prison cell deep in a castle.

According to Adolphe-Alexander Dillens's mid-1800s painting of Joan, she displayed strength even during her capture.

Comme il se mestoit alabzy.
Pour regarder dessus la ville.

Il luy vint dire vng de ses gens.
Monseigneur vous pouez a plain.

This fifteenth-century Martial d'Auvergne miniature imagines the siege of Orléans.

FROM CANNONS TO COLUMBUS

The Hundred Years' War, which stretched from the 1300s into the 1400s, was a "military revolution," notably in the artillery that became popular immediately before, during, and after the war.

The Chinese invented gunpowder hundreds of years before the chemical explosive arrived in Europe. The Europeans were quick to catch up with the technology, making use of their skills in metal casting in combination with the gunpowder to create cannons. In 1333, the first European cannon was used in the siege of Berwick.

The English, under Edward III, first turned a cannon on France in 1346. It took France until 1375 to acquire their own cannons for use against the English, but when they did, they hit back with a roar many soldiers had never heard previously: the sound of thirty-two cannons firing from around Saint-Sauveur-le-Vicomte must have been disorienting and terrifying.

This was a stunning advancement because the weaponry could lay waste to the city walls like no artillery before it could. Walls had been built with height rather than width in mind to prevent the enemy from scaling them. Now, because of cannons, walls would have to be rebuilt with thickness and durability as the focus.

Take also for example the famous fall of Constantinople, the largest European city for a millennium, serving as the center of trade between Europe and Asia. It was also the seat of Christianity.

In 1453, the Ottoman Turks conquered the city, claiming its power and riches as their own. They managed the previously unthinkable by using cannons.

Suddenly, walls meant nothing. This mattered physically but also mentally. The fall of Constantinople introduced a new psychological terror. There was nowhere to hide.

The Turks raised prices on spices, silk, and porcelain. Desperate for the luxury goods they were accustomed to having but at prices they were willing to pay, the Europeans focused their efforts on the sea, to develop new trade routes across the ocean. The fall of Constantinople is related to Christopher Columbus's famous voyage; he set out when he did, with the support of his country, because they were creating trade routes.

CHAPTER FOUR

The Aftermath *of* Joan's War

J oan was killed by the Inquisition," George Bernard Shaw wrote in 1931. "The Inquisition is still with us." This famous author, and an admirer of Joan who wrote a play about her in 1923, likely was referencing both the infamous commissions that sussed out heresy with torture in the thirteenth century and the attitudes behind them. When he wrote those words on the eve of Nazi Germany's rise to power, "he believed that when a country fell too far behindhand with its political institutions you were likely to get dictatorships, and when you get dictatorships you will get secret tribunals dealing with sedition and political heresy," Shaw's biographer explained.

Joan of Arc didn't have to die like she did. She was the victim of complicated attitudes in a complicated time.

Opposite: Though Charles VII is being crowned, Joan is at the center of attention in this 1854 painting by Jean-August-Dominque Ingres.

Joan's Trial

Forty-two clerics from theological and legal fields gathered in the chapel of Rouen's fortress on February 21, 1431. Joan, dressed as a boy, stood before them. She had been checked, once again, to confirm her physical purity, and now she was ready for her verbal trial. To begin, the investigators read aloud:

> ...This woman, utterly disregarding what is honourable in the female sex, breaking the bounds of modesty, and forgetting all feminine decency, has disgracefully put on the clothing of the male sex, a shocking and vile monstrosity. And what is more, her presumption went so far that she dared to do, say and disseminate many things beyond and contrary to the Catholic faith...

After months in prison as the only woman among men who did not speak her language, Joan now had to stand before more men and be questioned about everything: her childhood, her family, her voices, her choices as a soldier. Throughout it all, she did not waver.

At the end of day one, Joan complained of the iron leg restraints they forced her to wear. When Bishop Cauchon, leading the trial, reminded her that she had tried to escape, twice, she responded that the desire to escape was every captive's right. Perhaps, she suggested, they should not be asking her to pledge not to try to flee but asking her guards to "swear on the gospels that they would guard her well."

At the beginning of the second day, she balked at swearing to tell the truth because she'd already taken such an oath the day before. "You burden me too much," she said. She was on trial for her life, and Joan was determined to maintain her dignity in all matters. Every day, she would protest the request that she renew her promise to tell the truth.

Sometimes Joan outright refused to answer. When asked if it had been right of her to attack Paris on the Virgin Mary's feast day, Joan told them to keep moving the questioning along.

When one of her interrogators asked her, in a thick accent that betrayed his home region, what language her voices spoke, she retorted that they spoke French far better than he did.

The numbers of clerics in attendance grew with each session. By the third, there were sixty-two pressing for space. They asked when she had last heard voices. That very morning, she said, they had woken her from her slumber to tell her to "answer you boldly."

They demanded she ask the voice to deliver a message to the king. They couldn't argue with her response, which was that the voice would do so only if it were God's will. They asked her about the fairy tree, and Joan said her flower garlands were for the Virgin and that she danced only near the tree.

Joan's Trial

On March 18, Bishop Cauchon decided that accusations could be drawn up based on Joan's testimony. Yes, Joan's own answers informed her jailers of what they thought she'd done wrong. Of the seventy charges first brought against her, which ranged from sorcery to horse theft, by early April 1431, only twelve complaints remained, most related to her wearing of men's clothing and claims that God had directly contacted her. She preferred the wrong mode of dress for her gender, a sin according to the Catholic religion and illegal according to French law, and she had behaved contrary to Christian doctrine.

The Maid of Orléans stands trial.

On May 23, the young theologian Pierre Maurice, closer than the others to being Joan's contemporary, read through the twelve complaints: she'd clearly either made up the voices or if she hadn't, they were from the devil. Her claim to know the future was boastful. Her clothing was against nature. She had encouraged war. When she left home in secret, she had not honored her parents. Her leap from the Beaurevoir tower was an attempt at the greatest sin, suicide. Finally, by "refusing to submit to the judgement of God's Church on earth, she had withdrawn herself from the community of the faithful." In closing, he begged her, as a "dearest friend," to think carefully about if she would confess or resist. Bishop Cauchon, instrumental in the negotiation for Joan from the Burgundians and a lead in her trial, told her they would spare her the death penalty if only she would confess. He wanted to save a life as well as a soul. She refused.

On May 24, they took her, blinking, into the light of the abbey of Saint-Ouen to have her sentence read publicly. She made an appeal to Rome: they should take her case to the pope, and she would agree with what he decided. No, they said; that's too far away, and the only judges that mattered were the ones before her. They announced the order to execute her. At that, Joan spoke again. She repented. The bishop breathed a sigh of relief that he had saved a life as well as a soul. Many of the people gathered were angry that the horrible woman would not be killed for her sins. Back in her cell, Joan immediately exchanged her boy clothes for a dress and allowed her head to be shaved.

The End—and a Beginning

It's up for debate whether Joan fully understood what she was signing, but it's a moot point in the end: on May 28, Bishop

This painting shows Joan tied to the stake.

Cauchon was called to Joan's cell. She was dressed as a boy. She recanted her confession, explaining that the voices had told her she "had damned her soul to save her life." She agreed with them and wanted to make things right.

There was no turning back from the "relapsed heretic" conviction now given her—she was sent to the stake. On May 30, her accusers gave her a pointed hat that had the words "relapsed heretic, apostate, idolater" written on it. They put her in a cart and drove her through the crowded streets to the site of execution. Before a crowd of ten thousand, soldiers held her and bound her to the stake. There was a sermon and another reading of her sins.

She prayed, "Jesus, Jesus, Jesus," which were her last words before death.

Once the first fire had done its job, the **Cardinal** of Winchester ordered her remains to be burned a second time. Picking through what was left, they saw that her organs still survived, so a third burning was ordered to destroy the body completely. Joan's now decimated remains and the cinders from the fire that destroyed her were thrown into the River Seine.

Joan's Trial is Put on Trial

Of the forty-two lawyers who'd heard Joan's testimony, thirty-nine had asked she be granted leniency. In time, King Charles VI agreed that something had to be done to correct the wrong done to Joan.

Joan's mother, who had moved to Orléans in 1440 and received a pension from the city in thanks for her daughter's service, would stand in Joan's place in the investigation of her trial, along with Joan's brothers Pierre and Jean. On November 7, 1455, in Notre Dame in Paris, this nullification process began. This time the inquisitors looked to many witnesses who could speak to her childhood and her times in battle. Eight months later to the day, on July 7, 1456, the judges declared that the truth "had been passed over in silence," as Castor put it. The final twelve charges themselves had been created, the judges said, "corruptly, deceitfully, slanderously, fraudulently and maliciously." Joan was pardoned for sins she had never committed but of which she had been convicted. The wheels would start to turn to make her a saint. On May 16, 1920, more than sixty thousand people attended Joan's canonization ceremony at St. Peter's Basilica in Rome.

One Final Skirmish Across the Channel

The hostilities between England and France over the centuries have been brutal, claiming many lives and building deep resentment. It can be argued that they were locked in battle, physical warfare or cold wars, from the Norman Conquest of 1066 to the Entente Cordiale, a truce between the two, in 1904. The two countries began to find themselves on the same side of many world affairs and made peace with each other. Still, according to what historian Jose-Alain Fralon of France told the Associated Press in 2007, the British are France's "most dear enemies."

And when it comes to Joan of Arc—France's heroine, executed by England—the tension between the two countries may never be eased. In 2016, ownership of a gold-plated silver ring thought to have belonged to Joan of Arc brought England and France to harsh words.

After Joan's execution, Cardinal Henry Beaufort took possession of the ring Joan always wore, which had been a gift from her parents. No one knew its fate until Beaufort's descendant Lady Ottoline Morrell announced around the time of Joan's **beatification** in 1909 that the ring still existed. No longer would it pass from generation to generation—through gifts and sales, it began to move around England.

In 1947, it sold at a Sotheby's auction to a doctor; when he died, it passed to his son, who'd casually played with it as a child, even though the family was well aware of the ring's history. "My earliest memory of it was when I was about four years old when my sister was wearing the ring and [she] and I reenacted the battle when the British defeated Joan of Arc and captured her," Robert Hasson said in a video produced by Timeline Auctions, which conducted the bidding for the ring when Hasson sold it on February 26, 2016.

The fight for ownership was fierce; the winning bid was $425,000, nearly thirty times the starting bid. Le Puy du Fou, a theme park in France that allows people to explore historical events, brought the ring back to its home soil after nearly six hundred years being "held prisoner in England," the theme park president, Nicolas de Villiers, told the British newspaper the *Guardian*. De Villiers hoped the reclaiming of a "symbol of hope and victory" that had been worn by a "great woman" would "help the French rediscover the pride and confidence that they have lost today." Five thousand people attended the ceremony to welcome the ring back to France.

And then things threatened to turn ugly.

The British National Arts Council sent de Villiers a letter stating that the ring should be returned to England because de Villiers had failed to obtain the correct export license. Even if the new owner agreed to address Britain's letter, there was fear that a British buyer would step in, bid, and win the ring, allowed under the law.

De Villiers's father, Philippe, a prominent right-leaning politician, said, "Ladies and gentlemen from Britain, if you want to see the ring, then come to the Puy de Fou … The ring has returned to France and here it will stay … even if the European Commission orders it back."

His son wrote directly to the Queen of England, and the argument fell from its crest. The British government rescinded its complaint.

As of August, the theme park was planning to build a chapel to house the ring and welcome viewers to see this symbol of national pride and important religious artifact free of charge.

Of course, as the *Economist* and its interviewed experts pointed out, without wills, letters, inventories, or other such documentation, the ring doesn't have the provenance experts usually demand of artifacts. The unquestioning acceptance of this ring as Joan's puts people today at risk of falling into the

Joan of Arc may have worn this very ring.

same Joan of Arc mania that swept the nineteenth and twentieth centuries, around her beatification and canonization.

Joan as a Political Symbol

To accept this ring as Joan of Arc's if it did not belong to her potentially has consequences beyond the embarrassment of misdirected admiration. De Villiers has said that "Joan belongs to all French," but she has been claimed, across time and place, by multiple movements and groups as their own. People of a variety of beliefs have assumed Joan fits with their ideals. A clear example of this can be found by looking at World War II. Both Vichy France and the French resistance, who were enemies of each other, on complete opposite sides in the war, claimed Joan of Arc as a symbol for their cause.

Not all claims on Joan are as starkly contradictory as that one, though a diversity of groups have admired her independently of one another. Some people who have been called their country's or their movement's Joan of Arc have worked on behalf of their faith, as Joan did. Some have died for their beliefs, as Joan did. All who have been given that name have been fighters. Of all of Joan's defining characteristics, strong leadership is what people focus on when they think of Joan.

Joan as a Xenophobe

National pride can too easily slip into intense, irrational hatred of people from other countries, and today's politically centrist and left-leaning French people worry that the far right has claimed Joan of Arc, who so loved her country, exclusively for its own. Every May 1, the National Front (a right-wing, nationalist

Ani Pachen Dolma was a Buddhist nun who advocated for Tibetan freedom.

party) gathers at her statue in Paris, and its leader, Marine le Pen, tweeted a thanks to the de Villiers family "for bringing Joan of Arc's ring back to French soil." In 2016, the right and the left argued when elementary school curriculum changed across the country, removing emphasis on Joan of Arc. The federal education minister is in charge of school programs nationwide. The current minister is socialist and sees education as, most importantly, a reflection of the changes in society, while right-leaning leaders believe it should foster national pride.

Joan as Afghan Warrior

Malala Yousafzai, a contemporary young hero, was named for the Afghan Joan of Arc, Malalai of Maiwand. During the Second Anglo-Afghan War, Malalai led her people to victory over the British empire in the Battle of Maiwand in July 1880. The Afghan forces were beaten back by the British military's artillery—until Malalai took up arms. "Young love!" she shouted to the downtrodden soldiers. "If you do not fall in the battle of Maiwand, by God, someone is saving you as a symbol of shame!" Invigorated, they surged forward. One of the flag-bearers fell, and Malalai took up his flag (some accounts say she made a flag of her veil). She was killed, but because of her bravery and leadership, and her people's eventual win that day, she was **martyred**. Schools and hospitals have been named for her, and her grave has become a place for pilgrims to visit.

Joan as Albanian Fighter

A 1911 *New York Times* article nicknamed Tringe Smajl Martini the Albanian Joan of Arc for her role in resisting the army of the

Ottoman Empire. Born in 1880, she was a young woman, dressed as a man, when she fought her people's enemy after they captured and killed her father and brothers. She died quietly in 1917, after years of fighting and being imprisoned, and was buried near her family in the mountains of Gruda in what is now Montenegro. The grave is unmarked, her tombstone having been destroyed in a raid. Still today she is celebrated as a people's hero in Albania, with several streets in both Albania and Kosovo named for her.

Joan as a Mexican Rebel

Tens of thousands of people died during the Cristero War, or Cristero Rebellion, during which Roman Catholics, persecuted by the federal government, rose up. More than two dozen saints and martyrs came out of the conflict, some of whom claimed an earlier saint as their inspiration.

Female government resistors belonged to the Feminine Brigades of Saint Joan of Arc, performing many duties alongside the men. One of the major ones was manufacturing or otherwise obtaining ammunition to distribute to the troops. Field commanders credited them with the rebels lasting as long as they did.

Jovita Valdovinos was one of these women. Like her medieval French counterpart, this twentieth-century "Mexican Joan of Arc" was born in the countryside in 1911. Valdovinos witnessed the Mexican government violently outlaw religion in the wake of the Mexican Revolution (1910–1920). They not only shut churches down but killed priests and practitioners. Her father commanded a battalion against the Federation Army, one of her brothers was killed, and Valdovinos, then fifteen years old, was captured, raped by a Federation general, and shot. She survived and escaped her captors, but her torment wasn't complete.

The Federation hunted down resistance fighters, such as Valdovinos's father and another of her brothers. Valdovinos knew she had to act.

She began answering to the name Juan and, like Joan of Arc, cut her hair short and donned a man's typical outfit, in this case, denim overalls, long-sleeved cotton shirt, and a wide-brimmed straw hat. Eighty men followed her as she rode on her stallion, her dog by her side, into the rugged Sierra de Morones. She sought not help for Catholicism so much as she did revenge for her family, and her story also ended much differently than Joan's: after five years of fighting, Valdovinos accepted the government's offer of a truce, and the president pardoned her and even gave her a monetary reward. She lived into her nineties, but like Joan, she's been appreciated and vilified for her service.

Joan as Buddhist Nun

Born around 1933, Pachen Dolma wanted to devote her life to Buddhism. She even came to be known as Ani Pachen, Nun Big Courage, as well as the Tibetan Joan of Arc. Politics and war would set her on a different path. In 1958, she assumed her father's leadership role in her Tibetan village after he died. The Chinese were trying to take control, and the Tibetan resistance needed her leadership. She was captured nearly two years later. When her captors realized she did not fear death, they imprisoned her. Over twenty-one years in captivity, she lived through many horrible things, including a year in leg irons and a week being hung by her wrists. She and her fellow inmates faced severe starvation—she said she "would rejoice" when she found a worm. She stayed sane during nine months of solitary confinement by focusing on her faith and setting a goal to complete one hundred thousand ritual prostrations. In the end, she said, "I felt terrible for those who imprisoned me, believing that their actions in this life resulted from karma from their past lives."

From her release in 1981 to her death in 2002, she fought for human rights for Tibetan people.

Joan as Vivandiere

Women, often daughters or wives of officers, accompanied military regiments during the American Civil War, providing medical and other support. Eighteen-year-old Sarah Taylor was a vivandiere with the First Tennessee, her stepfather's regiment. It's been said that a letter from camp talked about Taylor, noting her "fantastically arranged" hair beneath her cap and her "highly-finished regulation sword, and silver-mounted pistols in her belt." She was the "second Joan of Arc." At least one scholar, Alice Fahs, called this "sensational fiction," pointing to the "circular dynamic within the commercial literary culture of the war. Sensational fiction often provided a language for representations of the war's events—and the resulting representations were often then used as the 'factual' basis for sensational fiction."

The original Joan of Arc and the Joans of later years had much in common indeed, including all the stories surrounding them.

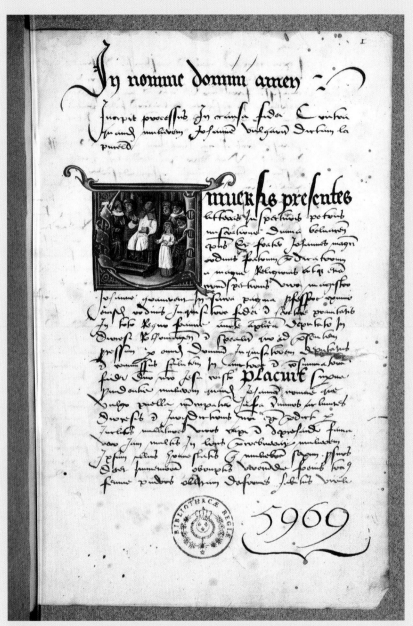

This is a page from the transcripts of the trial of Joan of Arc.

STRONG UNDER THREAT OF TORTURE

The following is an excerpt from Joan of Arc's trial transcript. It shows how fearless this nineteen-year-old was.

In the same year, Wednesday May 9, Joan was brought before us, the judges, in the great tower of the castle of Rouen...

Then Joan was requested and advised to tell the truth about many different matters in her trial that she had denied earlier or had lied about, in the face of positive information, proofs, and overwhelming presumptions. Many of these were read and explained to her, and she was told that if she would not confess the truth about them, she would be put to the torture, and she was shown the instruments ready in the tower. Officers were also present who were ready to put her to the torture, upon our order, so as to lead her back to the path and knowledge of the truth, and thereby save her soul and body, which, by her false stories, she had exposed to grave dangers.

Joan answered: "In truth, if you tear my limbs apart and separate my soul from my body, I still won't tell you anything else. And if I tell you anything, later I will say that you forced it out of me."

...

Seeing the hardness of her heart and the tone of her answers, we the judges feared that the instruments of torture would profit her little, and decided not to apply them until we had further counsel on the matter.

CHAPTER FIVE

Myths, Legends, *and* Popular Culture

*C*ourageous, *religious*, *brave*—in addition to all those adjectives to describe Joan of Arc, *mythical* must also be included. People don't know what to believe about her; some scholars have even claimed she wasn't real. While that perspective has been widely rejected, throughout the years there have been lots of lies, theories, and imaginative interpretations of her life.

"By the nineteenth century," Michael Holroyd, the well-regarded British biographer, wrote in the *Guardian* newspaper, "Joan of Arc had become public property." Both secular and religious groups grabbed at her story—she was a national hero, a military star, a feminist icon, and a martyr in service to God with unwavering faith.

Opposite: One of the most interesting things about Jeanne Jacquenin's portrait of the Maid of Orléans is Joan's long hair.

Secret Birth and Faked Death

In 1819, Pierre Caze argued in his *La Vérité sur Jeanne d'Arc* that Joan was secretly part of the royal family, born to Queen Isabeau of Bavaria and Duke Louis of Orléans. They placed her with the d'Arc family with instructions on the secret sign Joan should give Charles VII, her half-brother, should they reunite, so they would know each other.

Caze liked this theory because it helped to explain Charles VII's quick trust in her. Supporting this theory were the facts that there had been rumors that the queen and the duke had had an affair. And Joan's voices had told her, "When you stand before the king, he will have a sign [that will make him] receive you and believe in you."

There are either great problems with the timeline, or lots of people were in on an elaborate scheme to hide Joan's lineage—evidence supports neither. The queen delivered a son on November 10, 1407; the duke died two weeks later. Even if a daughter, Joan, was conceived in that short time, she would be twenty-three at the time of her death, and everyone, including Joan, agreed that she was nineteen in 1431.

Some people do not want to believe Joan died when and as she did. It has been suggested that someone else was burned at the stake in Joan's place. Claude des Armoises was the most famous subject of these rumors. She collaborated with Joan's brothers, Jean and Pierre, in the scheme to fool the people of Orléans, receiving in the process expensive gifts and party after party. Des Armoises finally admitted the ruse.

Modern-Day Diagnoses

Mainstream Western society in the twenty-first century seeks a scientific, rather than spiritual, explanation for the voices and visions Joan claimed came from God, and there are many modern theories. Experts have suggested that Joan had a neurological or psychiatric condition that triggered hallucinations or delusions. Migraines, brain lesions, and bipolar disorder, among others, can cause such symptoms. In May 2016, a neurologist and a professor of biomedical and neuromotor sciences, both from Italy, published a piece suggesting that Joan had idiopathic partial epilepsy with auditory features (IPEAF). Auditory and visual hallucinations can be symptoms of this type of epilepsy, as can hallucinations occurring during sleep, which Joan experienced. The high frequency with which Joan experienced the voices, however, is not common with this type of epilepsy. Scientists have found genetic connections to epilepsy, so these researchers are hoping get their hands on Joan's DNA. She was known to have sealed some of her letters with red wax into which she pressed her fingerprint and a strand of her hair. If they could find those, they could test the DNA of the hair to see if she had genes predisposed to IPEAF.

Or Joan may have experienced something people today no longer worry about. For example, as a young girl, she tended cattle and drank unpasteurized milk (pasteurization was a French invention, but Louis Pasteur wouldn't devise it until four hundred years after Joan lived). From that exposure to cows and untreated dairy, she might have picked up bovine tuberculosis, which can cause seizures and dementia.

In short, as the IPEAF researchers wrote, "after six hundred years from Joan's death, we reaffirm the impossibility to arrive at a final conclusion."

Joan in Popular Culture

Joan's popularity soared during times of French pride, like the Restoration of the Monarchy (1814–1830) and the July Monarchy (1830–1848). After the Franco-Prussian war (1870–1871), schools were named after her. Now that many people claim her as their own, Joan's likeness is used whenever and wherever, for no particular reason at all except that her strength and intrigue never seem to go out of style.

Joan in Advertising

In perhaps the most blatant example of her property, in the wake of the Franco-Prussian war, her image was used to sell everything from alcohol and cheese to fabric and perfume.

She remains an advertising darling: in 1988, clothing company Benetton, known for its United Colors of Benetton campaign, launched a United Superstars of Benetton, pairing legends from different eras, like Joan of Arc with Marilyn Monroe. In 2010 commercials for Poise underwear, Whoopi Goldberg's Joan-based character worried about light incontinence as she stood tied to the stake; if only she had Poise underwear protection, she wouldn't worry about being so scared of burning alive that she wet her pants.

Joan of Arc's Hair

In 1909, *the* stylist of the Paris fashion scene introduced Joan of

Joan's haircut was the clear inspiration for the classic bob hairstyle.

Arc's haircut as the 'do to do. Monsieur Antoine gave his clients "bobs," crediting Joan of Arc as his inspiration. The trend found widespread popularity in the 1920s—flappers and many silent-movie stars sported the style—and it's still common today.

Joan of Arc in Art

Poets, playwrights, painters, directors, actors, dancers, musicians, sculptors, artists of all types have loved exploring the story of the Maid of Orléans for nearly six hundred years. Just as myth surrounds her life, mixed interpretations swirl around many of these works of art. Still, whatever her truth, Joan is thought to be known. She's so well-known that even popular television shows will make passing reference to her. A remark in a 1979 episode of the long-running series *M*A*S*H* does a nice job of summarizing Joan's pervasive presence in even modern society.

On the show, the 4077th, a surgical unit in the Korean War, is caught in a major crossfire. But Hawkeye, a surgeon, and Margaret, a nurse, must operate on a patient whose health is deteriorating rapidly. Hawkeye suggests a game of Twenty Questions to calm Margaret's nerves. Margaret thinks of a famous person Hawkeye must guess the identity of by asking yes-no questions. At the end of the surgery, Hawkeye guesses Joan of Arc. They had been surrounded by exploding bombs and focused on saving their patient's life, but he jokes that he guessed correctly because "who else would you be thinking of?"

It's a short reference, but the writers trusted the audience to understand. Maybe the viewers would connect Joan's violent life with the situation these two characters, half a millennium later, found themselves in. Maybe they'd appreciate the strong character of Margaret thinking of a strong feminine icon during one of the most frightening moments of Margaret's life. Or maybe they'd just recognize Joan of Arc's name as that of someone incredibly famous but removed from the situation at hand and understand that the television show was highlighting the ludicrousness of the situation.

Because Joan of Arc has been the focus of so many works of art over the years, and the subject of passing mentions in quite a few others, they can't all be listed here. But following are some of the many highlights. In a 2017 article, then president Barack Obama shared that he considers art "a reminder of the truths under the surface of what we argue about every day." There are things to be learned about the true Joan—and the world that she lived in—from each of these.

Joan of Arc in Literature

Poets, playwrights, and novelists alike have written about Joan. Some have described her with earnest devotion, others with acerbic commentary. Some told her story in relatively

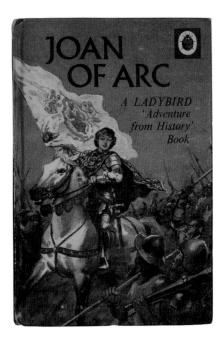

Joan of Arc's story has inspired many authors.

straightforward manners; others have reimagined her taking a variety of forms, including an alien predator.

The Song of Joan of Arc

Within Joan's lifetime, only one popular piece of writing was dedicated to her story—and a woman wrote it. Born in Venice around 1364 but living most of her life in France, Christine de Pisan was a professional writer employed by the French royal court, an incredibly unusual position for a woman to hold. Her father was French King Charles V's physician and astrologer and felt it was important that de Pisan, even though she was a girl, be educated. This came in handy when de Pisan's husband died, and she had to work to support her children. She wrote Charles V's official biography and then became the first female court historian. In this role, she wrote everything from manuals for war to poems. She also used her position to write several works about women being equal to men and documented the lives of several heroic women. It makes sense, then, that she'd be drawn to Joan's story.

In 1418, when the Burgundians took control of Paris, she left for an abbey outside the city, silenced by fear over the state of affairs. When she heard about Joan, de Pisan stepped into public again. She declared, now as joyful as she had been grief-stricken, that God had given Joan "a heart greater than any man's."

The Song of Joan of Arc, a ballad, was her project for her official retirement years; it was published in 1429, about a year before she died.

"You have your country back in tow," de Pisan addressed King Charles VII in stanza fourteen, "Won back by wise Joan's mighty arm. / Thanks be to God, it happened so!" In stanza twenty-one, de Pisan praised Joan further:

> And you, blessed Maid, can we forget,
> Since God has honored you so much,
> Since you have sliced apart the rope
> That held us bound, with one sure touch?
> Could we praise you too much at all,
> When you have calmed our countryside,
> Once battered down by war's cruel blast,
> So that we may in peace reside?

Henry VI

During her trial, Joan referred to herself as Jehanne la Pucelle, Joan the Maid, and that is how William Shakespeare referred to her character in the first part of his play *Henry VI*, from 1592. Shakespeare follows her through her heroics and her death and through his other characters makes her out to be a witch and temptress of men.

The Maid of Orléans

Voltaire's parodic poem about Joan, *The Maid of Orléans*, was well read in the eighteenth and nineteenth centuries—and also banned, burned, and otherwise dismissed or destroyed because of its bawdiness. She may have been a warrior, the French author said with his work, but she was, at her core, a woman, a sexual being for men to ogle. Voltaire was known for not holding back when it came to writing about politically charged subjects, including his rejection of Joan's love, the Catholic Church.

The Personal Recollections of Joan of Arc

Mark Twain wrote a well-researched novel about Joan—he said he spent twelve years gathering information for it before he took another two years to write it. Though it's rarely mentioned today, he considered it his best work. "And besides," he said, "it furnished me seven times the pleasure afforded me by any of the others."

By the time in his career that this book was published, Twain was known for his humor, but this novel is somber. He also, by this time, hated Catholicism and France, but his book casts Joan in a favorable light, and he had nothing but the highest of praise for her. In a 1904 *Harper's* magazine essay, he called her "by far the most extraordinary person the human race has ever produced." He even quoted her in his essay "Last Words of Great Men" (1889). Though Joan was famous, research on her wasn't widely available to the mainstream. Historians consider Twain ahead of the times with his deep fascination.

Published as a serial in *Harper's* between April 1895 and April 1896, it is narrated by a fictionalized version of Joan's servant and scribe, Sieur Louis de Conte.

Saint Joan

Moved by his 1913 visit to the molded head of St. Maurice in Orléans, France, which locals believe was modeled after Joan of Arc, playwright George Bernard Shaw pledged to "do a Joan play some day." Ten years later, he did. The play celebrates Joan. "Joan's heresies and blasphemies are not heresies and blasphemies to us," Shaw wrote. "We sympathise with them. And she defends herself splendidly."

Saint Joan of the Stockyards

German playwright Bertolt Brecht reimagined Joan as Joan Dark, living in twentieth-century Chicago and fighting the owner of a meat-packing plant. It was first broadcast over the radio, in 1932, and it wasn't staged for a live audience till 1959, after Brecht's death.

Twenty-first Century Joans

In 2003, Terry Pratchett fictionalized Joan to lead an army in *Monstrous Regiment*, a book in his Discworld series. For her 2017 novel *The Book of Joan*, Lidia Yuknavitch reimagined Joan of Arc as a hero for a near-future Earth ravaged by world wars.

Joan of Arc in Dance, Sculpture, and Image

Visual depictions of Joan can be seen in both the living, breathing form of dance and in the permanence of busts, statues, paintings, and drawings.

Seraphic Dialogue

Created in 1955 by the twentieth-century dancer and choreographer Martha Graham, *Seraphic Dialogue* is a look at Joan through modern dance. Aided by three saints who are waiting for her to join them in canonization, Joan reviews her life, first as a maid, then as a warrior, and then as a martyr.

This is the only image of Joan produced during her lifetime.

Early Sketch of Joan

The earliest known drawing of Joan of Arc is a sketch of her by Clément de Fauquembergue, doodled in the margin of the register, or the diary, of the happenings of the Parliament of Paris on the day they received word of her Orléans victory. De Fauquembergue was the parliament secretary on May 10, 1429. He never saw her in person, but because he was her contemporary and worked in government and likely received reports on her, his picture is a welcome addition to how we see Joan. Though people like Voltaire emphasized Joan's femininity, de Fauquembergue made sure to highlight her sword and banner.

Joan Sat for a Painting

Joan of Arc actually sat for an artist to paint her likeness—unfortunately, that portrait did not survive. The closest we have is one produced between twenty and seventy years after her death and based on that since-destroyed original.

Looking for Joan in a Gauguin Fresco

Paul Gauguin's first fresco, or quickly executed painting on a plaster wall or ceiling, has come to be known as *Breton Girl Spinning*, but many have seen it as a depiction of Joan of Arc.

The oil painting was completed in 1889, its canvas the west wall of the dining room of the inn on the Breton coast of France where Gauguin lived for a year. There are many reasons that experts can't decide on the meaning behind the painting. The painting is part of a room of decorations that stretch across ceilings, doors, and even a window. Several other artists added

their touches to Gauguin's work. And in 1893, the innkeeper retired and moved, taking some of the room's paintings with her. *Breton Girl Spinning* stayed at the inn and, at the hands of future innkeepers, was wallpapered over. Rediscovered in 1924, it was owned privately until finding its home with the Van Gogh Museum in Amsterdam, Netherlands, in 2006.

People have thought they see Joan in the angel carrying a sword at the top of the painting, but scholars such as one of the foremost experts on the art at the inn don't believe that. Patriotism wasn't important to Gauguin, and it seems odd to place Joan in the context of the rest of the painting. Gauguin attended the Lycée Jeanne d'Arc for a year in 1864, but some experts say the angel looks clearly like Archangel Gabriel in pursuit of a sinner.

Statues in Orléans, New and Old

Discovered in 1827 in the ruins of the church of St-Maurice-St-Éloi in Orléans, France, the head of a statue from the turn of the sixteenth century has long been believed by many to have been modeled after Joan. Others think the statue was of St. George.

In 1964, French President Charles de Gaulle, with financial support from French cities Orléans, Paris, Rouen, and Reims, gave New Orleans, Louisiana, a statue of Joan of Arc. The gilded bronze statue of Joan on a horse was one of ten copies of the original plaster mold by Emmanuel Frémiet.

Opposite: In modern times, Joan of Arc rides through New Orleans.

Joan of Arc may have worn this helmet, now in the Metropolitan Museum of Art, into battle.

RELICS

Relics—physical remains or personal effects from venerated people—are important to people because they carry religious importance. They also serve as proof that people who have reached legend status lived and died. Though experts roundly agree that Joan of Arc lived, served as a military leader, and died at the stake, there will likely always be questions, even unfounded ones, because her story is so mythical, and she lived so long ago. As a result, people look for physical evidence of what happened to her.

Until 2007, scientists believed that a rib bone found at the site of Joan's execution was hers, a scrap of cloth had come from her gown, and, perhaps, that a cat bone was also from the fire that killed her. (Medieval practice included throwing a black cat into the fire set to kill an accused witch.) The items were in an apothecary until 1867, when they were moved from the pharmacy to the Tours, France **archdiocese** and then on to a museum in the town of Chinon. In 1909, scientists declared it "highly probable" that the relics were authentic. In 2006, scientists started reexamining them using modern techniques, and in December of that year believed they were "close to proving that controversial relics are actually those of the real-life Maid of Orleans." Four months later, they had declared "relatively little chance" of them being true relics. Though carbon dating showed the cloth was from the right century to have been worn by Joan, it wasn't burnt but dyed. The rib and cat bone were dated from the seventh to third centuries BCE, with the rib being from an Egyptian mummy.

Music about Joan

Patti Smith's song "Kimberly" (1975) includes the lines "The sea rushes up my knees like flame/And I feel like just some misplaced Joan of Arc." The theme song for the television show *Maude* (1972–1978) includes the line "Joan of Arc with the Lord to guide her/she was a sister who really cooked." And the Smiths' "Bigmouth Strikes Again" (1986) says, "And now I know how Joan of Arc felt, as the flames rose to her Roman nose and her Walkman started to melt," and "And now I know how Joan of Arc felt, as the flames rose to her Roman nose and her hearing aid started to melt."

Leonard Cohen's "Joan of Arc," from his third album, *Songs of Love and Hate* (1971), is a dialogue between Joan and the fire licking at her. Though people have wondered if the song's lyrics are saying that Joan needed a husband to be fulfilled, Cohen said in a 1988 interview with RTE Ireland that he meant not that she was looking for a bridegroom but that she had met and married her destiny. "From the point of view of the woman's movement she really does stand for something stunningly original and courageous." Earlier, in 1973, Cohen said in *New Musical Express*, "When I recorded that song I admit to having a strong religious feeling. I don't think it'll happen again."

Kate Bush is no stranger to writing and performing songs that recount the stories of legendary women. Her first single, "Wuthering Heights" (1978) retold Emily Brontë's novel. In 2005, she released a look at Joan of Arc's life with "Joanni." She couldn't ignore the connection she had with the song when, nine years later, she performed the song live. To accommodate the changes in her voice because of age, she changed the key of "Joanni." One of the members of her band had recorded cathedral bells in Rouen, France, where Joan was burned, and he played them at rehearsal.

On Madonna's 2015 album *Rebel Heart*, she sang about "Joan of Arc" because "women need female role models" who don't back down. Joan led her country to victory in battle, but people turned on her and allowed her to be executed. Still, she displayed her "elevated soul," standing firm in her journey.

Television and Movies about Joan

While *Wonderfalls*, a show about a recent college graduate who is guided by the voices of animal figurines to help others, lasted only the 2004 season, its creators had ideas for further seasons. Jaye Tyler's therapist was going to diagnose her with "Joan of Arc Syndrome," and Tyler would be institutionalized for the third season.

Joan of Arcadia ran for two seasons, 2003–2005, and was about high school student Joan Girardi, who could hear God and did as he asked in her hometown of Arcadia.

Joan the Woman was a 1916 silent film directed by Cecil B. DeMille, who is considered a founder of American cinema, and starring the famous opera singer and actor Geraldine Ferrar as Joan. The screenplay was based on Friedrich Schiller's 1801 play *The Maid of Orleans*. An officer in World War I dreams about Joan; upon waking, inspired by Joan, the officer rushes into battle.

In *Bill & Ted's Excellent Adventure*, Joan of Arc is one of many historical figures who time travel to 1980s Southern California. "Who was Joan of Arc?" a teacher asks. "Noah's wife?" Ted suggests. Later he says to her, "Welcome aboard, Miss of Arc," making a joke about translating "d'Arc" into English.

Video Games and Comics about Joan

Bayonetta (2010) is a videogame with Jeanne as a rival to Bayonetta; she wears a red dress from the fashion brand D'arc. *Deadliest Warrior: Legends* (2011) pits historical figures including Joan of Arc, against each other. Jeanne d'Arc is one of three main characters in the smartphone card action game *Angel Master*. The manga series Aria the Scarlet Ammo features Jeanne d'Arc 30, a descendant of the original Joan of Arc.

CHRONOLOGY

4TH CENTURY St. Peter's Basilica is built.

1339–1453 Hundred Years' War

1377 Popes start living in the Palace of the Vatican.

1412 Joan of Arc is born and baptized in Domrémy, northeastern France.

1415 King Henry V of England invades France.

1420 Under the Treaty of Troyes, King Henry V becomes regent for King Charles VI.

1422 Henry V and Charles VI die.

1425 Joan begins to hear voices.

1428 Joan tries to secure a meeting with the dauphin Charles; she is rejected.

1429 Joan is allowed to see Charles.

1429 Joan is put in charge of an army and goes on a multi-battle campaign for a total of seven weeks.

1429 The dauphin Charles becomes French King Charles VII.

1429 The king names Joan and her family as nobles.

1430 Joan is captured.

1431 Joan of Arc is tried for witchcraft and heresy and burned at the stake.

1450 Charles VII initiates an investigation into Joan's trial.

1453 The Ottoman Turks conquer Constantinople.

1456 The retrial of Joan of Arc.

16TH CENTURY Michelangelo's dome is added to St. Peter's Basilica.

1909 Joan of Arc is beatified.

1920 Joan of Arc is canonized.

1929 The Vatican City State is created as an independent nation.

GLOSSARY

APOSTLES The twelve disciples of Jesus Christ.

ARCHDIOCESE A diocese that is large, has historical importance, or both; is led by an archbishop.

ARTILLERY Large arms that fire munitions much farther than handheld guns.

BASILICA A church designated by the pope as special.

BASTILLE Jail.

BEATIFY A dead person who is a candidate for sainthood is blessed and may be venerated publicly.

BISHOP Ordained like a priest but of higher rank within the Catholic Church leadership; leads a diocese.

CANONIZE When a deceased person is declared to be a saint.

CARDINAL Appointed by the pope; one step lower in leadership from the pope.

CLERICAL Related to clergy.

CORONATION The ceremony to seal a monarch's ascension to power.

DAUPHIN The title given to the heir apparent to the French throne.

ECCLESIASTICAL Relating to Christianity or its clergy.

FORTIFY Strengthen a place in preparation for an attack.

FRESCO Painting on plaster, such as a wall or ceiling, produced quickly.

HOLY SEE The government of the Catholic Church.

MARTYR To kill someone because of that person's belief.

PILGRIMAGE A religious journey.

POPE Head of the Roman Catholic Church.

PRIEST Ordained minister of the Catholic Church.

REGENT A person who governs on behalf of the actual leader if that person is unable (for example, if the leader is too young to rule).

RELIC Physical remain or personal effect of saint.

THOUGHT-WORLD The combination of attitudes, beliefs, and presuppositions about the world that are characteristic of a people, time, or place.

FURTHER INFORMATION

BOOKS

Morris, Linda A. *Gender Play in Mark Twain: Cross-Dressing and Transgression*. Columbia, MO: University of Missouri, 2011.

Yousafzai, Malala. *I Am Malala: The Girl Who Stood Up for Education and Was Shot by the Taliban*. New York: Little, Brown and Company, 2013.

Yuknavitch, Lidia. *The Book of Joan*. New York: HarperCollins, 2017.

WEBSITES

Joan of Arcadia

http://www.imdb.com/title/tt0367345

Learn about *Joan of Arcadia*, a modern-day envisioning of the Joan of Arc legend, on the IMDB website.

Our Fake History

http://ourfakehistory.com/index.php/archived-episodes

Visit this website to learn about legends and myths, including a three-episode podcast on Joan of Arc.

VIDEO

Joan of Arc Phenomenon. Religion, and Ethics Newsweekly

http://www.pbs.org/video/2365019464

This seven-minute video is a nice blend of Joan of Arc's story and representations of Joan in modern society. Please note that it is a twenty-year-old video, and some language is outdated.

BIBLIOGRAPHY

Associated Press. "After Testing, Experts Say Rib Bone and Piece of Cloth Probably Are Not Remains of Joan of Arc." *Fox News*, December 16, 2006. http://www.foxnews.com/story/2006/12/16/after-testing-experts-say-rib-bone-and-piece-cloth-probably-are-not-remains.html.

———. "The European Union that Never Was." *NBC News*, January 15, 2007. http://www.nbcnews.com/id/16638084/ns/world_news-europe/t/european-union-never-was/#.WHkcMVxCi10.

———. "Joan of Arc's Bone? No, an Even Odder Tale." *New York Times*, April 5, 2007. http://www.nytimes.com/2007/04/05/world/europe/05bones.html.

Bie, Søren. "Jeanne's Family." Jeanne-darc.info. Accessed January 14, 2017. http://www.jeanne-darc.info/biography/family.

Biography.com Editors. "Joan of Arc Biography." Biography.com. October 6, 2016. http://www.biography.com/people/joan-of-arc-9354756.

Bos, Carole. "Joan of Arc—Medieval Painting." Awesomestories.com, October 7, 2013. https://www.awesomestories.com/asset/view/Joan-of-Arc-Medieval-Painting.

Castor, Helen. *Joan of Arc: A History.* New York: Harper/HarperCollins Publishers, 2015.

Catholic Online. "St. Catherine of Alexandria." Accessed January 14, 2015. http://www.catholic.org/saints/saint.php?saint_id=341.

————. "St. Margaret of Antioch." Accessed January 14, 2015. http://www.catholic.org/saints/saint.php?saint_id=199.

Cohen, Jennie. "7 Surprising Facts About Joan of Arc." History. com, January 28, 2013. http://www.history.com/news/history-lists/7-surprising-facts-about-joan-of-arc.

Crown, Daniel. "The Riddle of Mark Twain's Passion for Joan of Arc." *The Awl*, April 3, 2012. https://theawl.com/the-riddle-of-mark-twains-passion-for-joan-of-arc-8f20f997d13c.

Dalrymple, William. "Before Malala." *New York Times*, October 25, 2013. http://www.nytimes.com/2013/10/26/opinion/international/malalas-brave-namesake.html.

Donadio, Rachel. "Joan of Arc's Shaky Pedestal: France Battles Over Its Identity at School." *New York Times*, September 27, 2016. https://www.nytimes.com/2016/09/28/arts/joan-of-arcs-shaky-pedestal-france-battles-over-its-identity-at-school.html.

DrHGuy. "About those Songs on Leonard Cohen's Can't Forget Album: Joan of Arc—Part 1." Cohencentric.com, March 26, 2015. http://cohencentric.com/2015/03/26/about-those-songs-on-leonard-cohens-cant-forget-album-joan-of-arc-part-1/.

Editors of Encyclopaedia Britannica. "Saint Catherine of Alexandria." *Encyclopaedia Britannica*. Last updated December 16, 2010. https://www.britannica.com/biography/Saint-Catherine-of-Alexandria

Edward, "Women in the Civil War: Vivandieres." The Gilder Lehrman Institute of American History, March 12, 2012. https://www.gilderlehrman.org/community/blog/women-civil-war-vivandieres.

Fahs, Alice. *The Imagined Civil War: Popular Literature of the North and South, 1861–1865.* Chapel Hill, NC: University of North Carolina Press, 2003.

"File: Tete de Saint Maurice Orleans.jpg." Wikimedia Commons. Last updated January 6, 2017. https://commons.wikimedia. org/wiki/File:Tete_de_Saint_Maurice_Orleans.jpg.

Foreman, Amanda. "'Joan of Arc: A History,' by Helen Castor." *New York Times*, July 2, 2015. https://www.nytimes. com/2015/07/05/books/review/joan-of-arc-a-history-by-helen-castor.html?_r=0.

Gamble, Joan. "Domremy La Pucelle." *In Joan of Arc's Footsteps* (blog), October 25, 2012. http://injoanofarcsfootsteps.com/ articles/2012/10/domremy-la-pucelle.

Heiman, Nora M. "Spinner or Saint: Context and Meaning in Gaugin's First Fresco." *Nineteenth-Century Art Worldwide, 11*(2)(Summer 2012).

Hiatt, Brian. "Madonna on Making 'Rebel Heart,' the Age of Distraction and Joan of Arc." *Rolling Stone*, March 5, 2015. http://www.rollingstone.com/music/features/madonna-on-making-rebel-heart-the-age-of-distraction-and-joan-of-arc-20150305.

History.com Staff. "Joan of Arc." History.com, 2009. http://www. history.com/topics/saint-joan-of-arc.

Holroyd, Michael. "A Tragedy without Villains." *Guardian*, July 14, 2007. https://www.theguardian.com/books/2007/jul/14/ theatre.stage.

Jarus, Owen. "Joan of Arc: Facts & Biography." LiveScience, July 18, 2013. http://www.livescience.com/38288-joan-of-arc.html.

Joan of Arc. Ignatius Press. Accessed January 11, 2017. http:// www.ignatius.com/Products/JA-P/joan-of-arc.aspx.

"Joan of Arc Biography." *Encyclopedia of World Biography*. Accessed January 14, 2017. http://www.notablebiographies. com/Ho-Jo/Joan-of-Arc.html.

Kakutani, Michiko. "Obama's Secret to Surviving the White House Years: Books." *New York Times*, January 16, 2017. https://www.nytimes.com/2017/01/16/books/obamas-secret-to-surviving-the-white-house-years-books.html.

Kelly, Rob. "Episode 164—C*A*V*E." Aftermash.blogspot.com, September 17, 2009. http://aftermash.blogspot.com/2009/09/episode-164-cave.html.

Klein, Christopher. "Joan of Arc Ring Back in France After 600 Years in U.K." History.com, 2016. http://www.history.com/news/joan-of-arc-ring-back-in-france-after-600-years-in-u-k.

Knighton, Andrew. "How Artillery Evolved in the 100 Years War." *War History Online*, June 27, 2016. https://www.warhistoryonline.com/medieval/artillery-100-years-war.html.

Lay, Paul. "Interview: Helen Castor." *History Today*, June 16, 2011. http://www.historytoday.com/bookclub/interview-helen-castor.

Martin, Douglas. "Ani Pachen, Warrior Nun in Tibet Jail 21 Years, Dies." *New York Times*, February 18, 2002. http://www.nytimes.com/2002/02/18/world/ani-pachen-warrior-nun-in-tibet-jail-21-years-dies.html.

Mason, Emma. "7 Facts about the Hundred Years' War." *HistoryExtra*, October 22, 2015. http://www.historyextra.com/article/feature/seven-facts-about-hundred-years-war-agincourt.

Miller, Sara G. "What Really Caused the Voices in Joan of Arc's Head?" *LiveScience*. July 29, 2016. http://www.livescience.com/55597-joan-of-arc-voices-epilepsy.html.

Momand, Wahid. "Malalai of Maiwand." Afghanland.com, 2000. http://www.afghanland.com/history/malalai.html.

Nelson, Janet. "Joan of Arc by Helen Castor Review—A Triumph of History." *The Guardian*, October 29, 2014. https://www. theguardian.com/books/2014/oct/29/joan-of-arc-history-helen-castor-review-time.

O'Reilly, Don. "Hundred Years' War: Joan of Arc and the Siege of Orléans." Historynet.com. Originally in *Military History*, April 1998. http://www.historynet.com/joan-of-arc?PageSpeed=noscript.

Pareles, Jon. "Kate Bush Is Running Up That Concert Stage for a Giant Live Album." *New York Times*, November 24, 2016. https://www.nytimes.com/2016/11/24/arts/music/kate-bush-before-the-dawn-interview.html.

Paterson, Seale. "Moving Joan." *St. Charles Avenue*, March 2015. http://www.myneworleans.com/St-Charles-Avenue/March-2015/Moving-Joan/.

P. W. "The Twisting Tale of 'Joan of Arc's Ring.'" *Economist*, March 9, 2016. http://www.economist.com/blogs/prospero/2016/03/one-ring-fool-them-all.

Salas, Elizabeth. *Soldaderas in the Mexican Military: Myth and History*. Austin, TX: University of Texas, 1990.

Salazar, Aida. "My Aunt Was a Revolutionary General: Mexico's Joan of Arc." *Huffington Post*, April 12, 2016. http://www.huffingtonpost.com/aida-salazar/my-aunt-was-a-revolutionary_b_9645472.html.

Samuel, Henry. "'Come and Get It': French Refuse to Hand Joan of Arc's Ring Back to Britain." *Telegraph*, March 21, 2016. http://www.telegraph.co.uk/news/worldnews/europe/france/12200145/Come-and-get-it-French-refuse-to-hand-Joan-of-Arcs-ring-back-to-Britain.html.

Schaus, Margaret (Ed.). *Women and Gender in Medieval Europe: An Encyclopedia*. New York: Routledge, 2006.

Shopkow, Leah. "Joan of Arc: Documents." Indiana University. Accessed January 11, 2017. http://www.indiana.edu/~dmdhist/joan.htm.

Smith, Alex Duval. "Solved at Last: The Burning Mystery of Joan of Arc." *Guardian*, December 16, 2006. https://www.theguardian.com/world/2006/dec/17/france.alexduvalsmith.

Sojourn Photography. "Her Sword." Saintjoanofarc.com. Accessed January 16, 2017. http://saint-joan-of-arc.com/sword.htm.

SparkNotes Editors. "Joan of Arc." SparkNotes LLC, 2005. http://www.sparknotes.com/biography/joanofarc.

Warner, Marina. *Joan of Arc: The Image of Female Heroism.* Oxford, UK: Oxford University Press, 2013.

Willsher, Kim. "Joan of Arc Ring Stays in France After Appeal to Queen." *Guardian*, August 26, 2016. https://www.theguardian.com/world/2016/aug/26/joan-of-arc-ring-stays-in-france-after-appeal-to-queen.

Wind, Lee. *The Queer History Project: No Way, They Were Gay?* Hillsboro, OR: Beyond Words, 2017.

World Heritage Encyclopedia. "Tringe Smajl Martini." http://central.gutenberg.org/article/whebn0011380846/tringe%20smajl%20martini.

INDEX

Page numbers in **boldface** are illustrations. Entries in **boldface** are glossary terms.

trial, 6–7, 32, 34–36, 38,
48, 59, 67, 74-75, **76–
77,** 78-80, **90,** 91, 101
Troyes, 23, 60-61
Twain, Mark, 102

Vaucouleurs, 38–40
voices, 10, 17, 34, 36, **37,**
38–39, 48–49, 67, 74–
75, 78, 80, 94–95, 111

weaponry, 71

Yolande of Aragon, 25–26,
27, 32, 39–40, 42

ABOUT THE AUTHOR

KRISTIN THIEL is a writer and editor based in Portland, Oregon. She has written many books for Cavendish Square and other companies, including a book about chemist and X-ray crystallography pioneer Dorothy Hodgkin and titles in the So, You Want to Be A … series (Aladdin/Beyond Words), which offers career guidance for kids. She was the lead writer on a report for her city about funding for high school dropout prevention. Thiel has judged YA book contests and helped start a Kids Voting USA affiliate. She has been a substitute teacher in grades K–12 and managed before-school and afterschool literacy programs for AmeriCorps VISTA.